CAMBRIDGE
UNIVERSITY PRESS

CAMBRIDGE
Global English

for Cambridge Primary English as a Second Language

Learner's Book 6

Jane Boylan & Claire Medwell

Series Editor: Kathryn Harper

Contents

Contents

Writing/Projects	Use of English	Cross-curricular links	21st-century skills
Guided writing: Write a description of a first-time experience A presentation about something or someone special to you Design an 'Our names' poster for your classroom	Present perfect Prepositions before nouns	**Geography:** Where am I in the world?	Work collaboratively Describing what makes us feel happy, angry or excited **Critical thinking:** Exploring why an experience was special **Values:** Accepting our differences
Guided writing: Write a biography about a sports person Use quotes Make a poster about a type of sport Make a commentary of a sports event	First conditional with if/ unless need/should/ mustn't for advice	**Health education:** Eat for strength and energy	Work collaboratively Identify roles and responsibilities within a team Share ideas, information **Critical thinking:** Describe why we engage with different sports **Values:** Teamwork
Guided writing: Write an infographic about an animal A presentation about how an animal survives Create a quiz about an animal	Present simple Relative clauses Wh- questions review	**Natural science:** Nature's food chains	Develop empathy towards other children Work collaboratively **Critical thinking:** Explore how penguins survive in extreme temperatures Explain the survival habits of carnivorous plants **Values:** Feeling empathy
Guided writing: Write a persuasive essay about an invention Support your opinions	Past simple review Will for future predictions Multi-word verbs	**Design technology:** Radical robotics	Understand the importance and potential of creative thinking and self-belief Work collaboratively **Critical thinking:** Evaluate and express own opinions comparing different inventions **Values:** Believe in yourself

Contents

How to use this book

In this book you will find lots of different features to help your learning.

What you will learn in the unit or lesson.

> **We are going to...**
> - **talk** about different ways to spend money

Big questions to find out what you know already.

> **Getting started**
>
> What makes us who we are?
>
> a What activities and events can you see in the photos?
>   What activities and events are part of your world?
> b What do you think 'identity' is? What makes up your identity?
> c What do you have in common with the people around you?
>   What things are different?

The key words feature includes vocabulary from other subjects, Academic English terms and instruction words.

> **Key words: map reading**
>
> **pinpoint:** to find out or say the exact position
> **pole:** the most northern and southern points of the Earth
> **degree:** a unit of measurement
> **parallel:** two lines of equal distance apart
> **vertical:** standing upwards
> **coordinate:** a code with numbers and letters that shows exact positions on a map

At the end of each unit, there is a choice of projects to work on together, using what you have learned. You might do some research or make something.

> **⟩ 4.6 Project challenge**
>
> **Project A: A presentation about the history of an invention**
>
> 1 Work in a small group. Research the history of one of these inventions (or your own idea) using the internet or the library.

> 2 Plan your presentation! Make notes about:
>   - who invented it
>   - the first models

Questions to help you think about how you learn.

> What did you enjoy most about doing your project?

Language detective boxes help you find out more about the main grammar in a unit. ——————▶

> **Use of English – Present perfect**
>
> We use the present perfect tense to describe events in the recent past, when the time of the event is not important.
>
> *I have drawn a car...*

Helps you remember other grammar. ——————▶

> **Language focus – Verb patterns**
>
> Some verbs are followed by other words in a specific order:
>
> *... he **gave** me a funny smile...*
> verb + objects
>
> *My friend **asked** me to go with him...*
> verb + object + infinitive (with to)
>
> The **object** is the person/thing affected by the verb action.

Tips you can use to help you with your learning. ——————▶

> **Speaking tip**
>
> **Giving opinions and responding**
>
> So what do you think?
> No, I think it's better to...
> I think that's a good idea.
> Me too.
> Yes, that sounds right.
> I've got one more point to make. How about...?
> Great idea!

This is what you have learned in the unit. ——————▶

> **Look what I can do!**
>
> Write or show examples in your notebook.
>
> I can talk about feelings and compare with my friends.
> I can use the present perfect to talk about things that happened recently.
> I can find locations on a map using coordinates.
> I can use prepositional phrases to build sentences.
> I can do a presentation about someone I admire.
> I can describe a first-time experience.
> I can read and understand a story about a girl with an unusual name.

Games and activities that cover what you have learned in the previous three units. If you can answer these, you are ready to move on to the next unit. ——————▶

> # Check your progress 1
>
> 1 Read the clues and guess the words.
>
> a   This adjective means worried or anxious.
> b   This word describes the area around the street where you live.
> c   This noun means that you are pleased because you have done something good.
> d   You wear these to protect your eyes when you are swimming.
> e   This part of your body connects your foot to your leg.
> f   In football, this player stands by the net to stop the other team from scoring goals.
> g   A baby bird.

Audio is available with the Teacher's Resource or Digital Classroom. 🎧 10

Video is available with Digital Classroom. 🎥

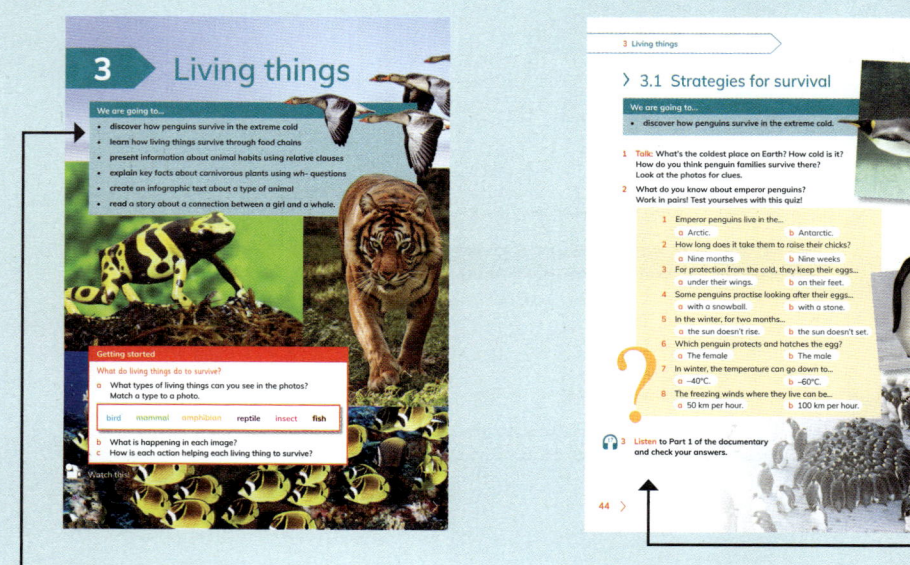

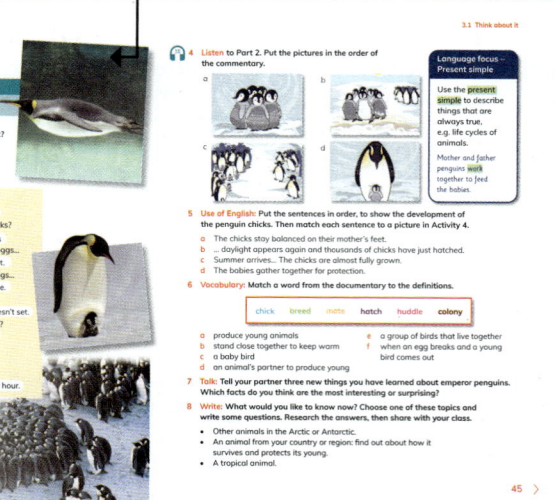

Lesson 1: The **Think about it** lesson introduces the topic through topic vocabulary activities.

Engage with the topic of the unit and generate discussion using the image, the video and the big question.

The opening lesson includes Listening.

Lesson 2: The **cross-curricular** lesson prepares learners to learn in English across the curriculum.

In this lesson you'll find Language Detective and Key Words boxes.

A non-fiction text exposes learners to cross-curricular language.

Grammar is presented through an active learning approach.

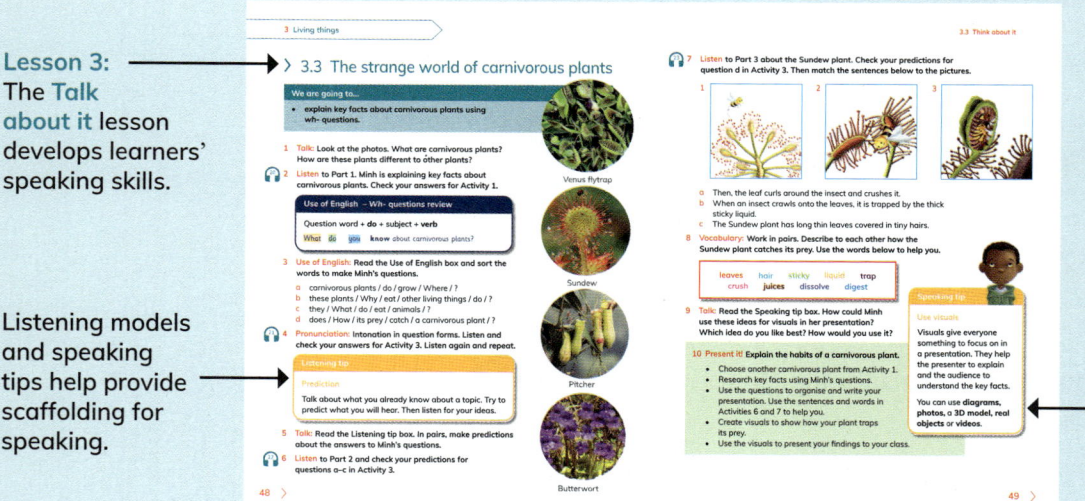

Lesson 3: The **Talk about it** lesson develops learners' speaking skills.

Listening models and speaking tips help provide scaffolding for speaking.

Pronunciation is supported through paired activities.

Lesson 4: The **Write about it** lesson supports learners to write effective texts.

Model texts with callouts support the writing process.

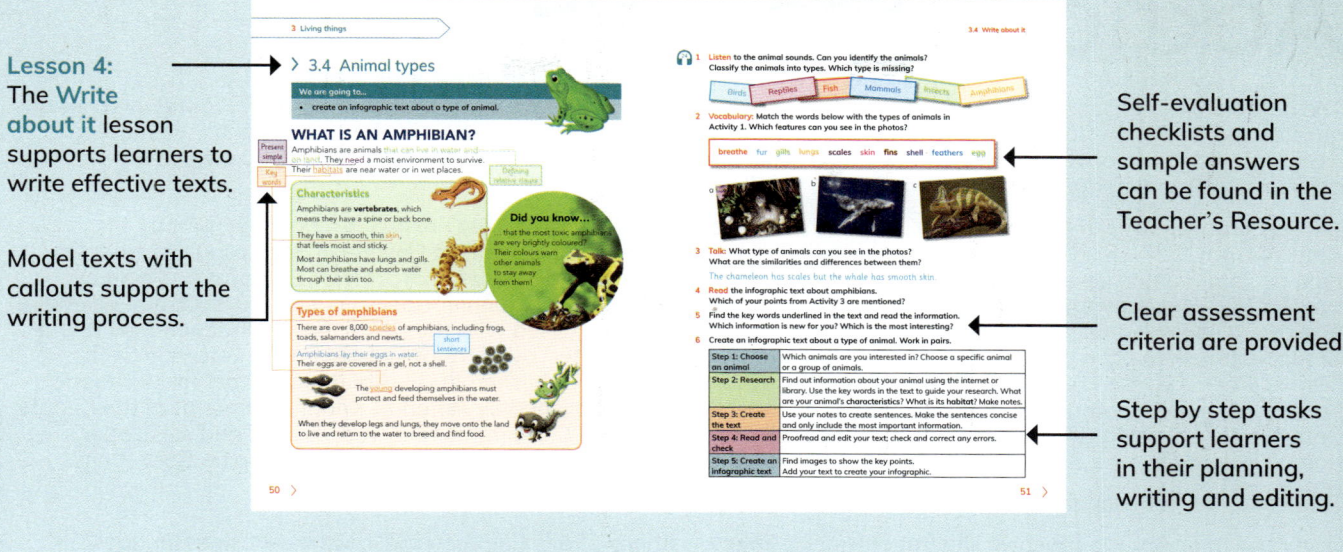

Self-evaluation checklists and sample answers can be found in the Teacher's Resource.

Clear assessment criteria are provided.

Step by step tasks support learners in their planning, writing and editing.

Lesson 5: The **Read and Respond** lesson includes literature. This might be a fictional story, a poem or a play.

The audio can be played the first time you meet the story, before learners read the text.

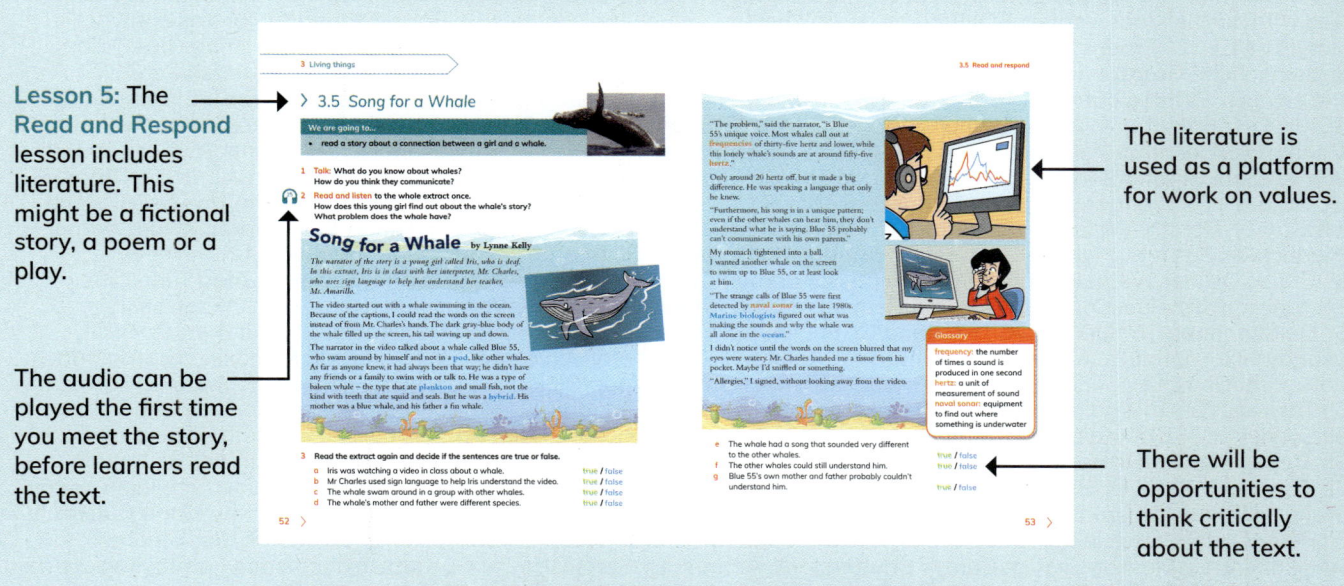

The literature is used as a platform for work on values.

There will be opportunities to think critically about the text.

Lesson 6: The **Project Challenge** lesson includes choice of projects.

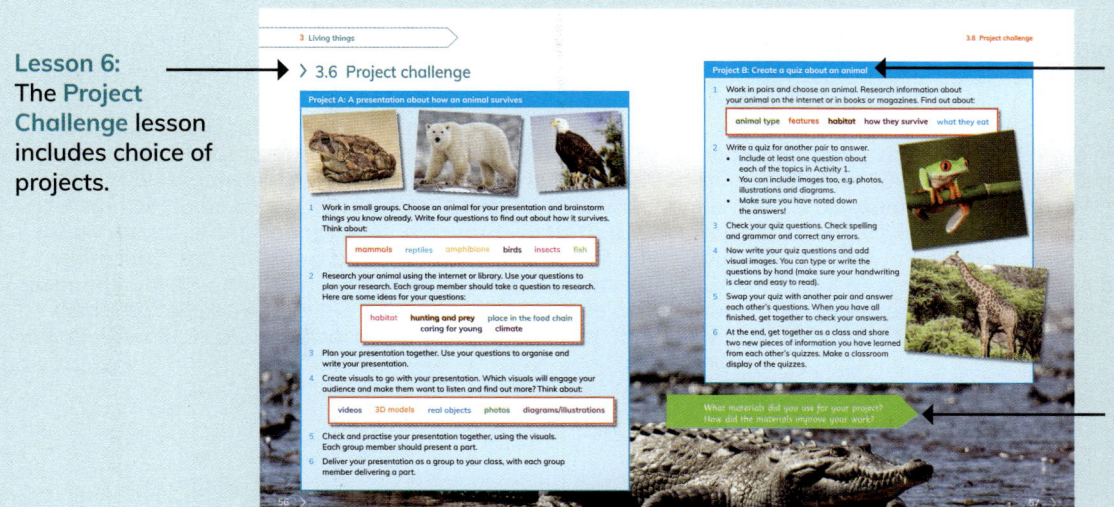

Projects encourage 21st-century skills such as research, collaboration, and creativity.

Self- and peer-evaluation checklists for projects are available in the Teacher's Resource.

Acknowledgements

The authors and publishers acknowledge the following sources of copyright material and are grateful for the permissions granted. While every effort has been made, it has not always been possible to identify the sources of all the material used, or to trace all copyright holders. If any omissions are brought to our notice, we will be happy to include the appropriate acknowledgements on reprinting.

Text excerpt from *A Girl Called Owl* by Amy Wilson (also published as *The Lost Frost Girl*) Text Copyright by Amy Wilson 2017. Used by permission of HarperCollins Publishers and Macmillan Children's Books; Extract from *Off Side* by Tom Palmer. Used with the permission of Random House Group Limited; Extract from *Song for a Whale* by Lynne Kelly. Text copyright Lynne Kelly, 2019. First published in the UK by Bonnier Books UK Ltd; Extract from *Billionaire Boy* by David Walliams, published by HarperCollins Children's Books. Used with the permission of Independent Talent Group Limited; 'You can be anything' by Teri Hopkins; 'Thank-You Letter' by Eric Finney from *Loony Letters & Daft Diaries: Poems chosen by Paul Cookson*, Macmillan Children's Books Published 2003; Abridged extract from *Jurassic Park* by Michael Crichton, Copyright © 1990 by Michael Crichton, published by Alfred A. Knopf, an imprint of the Knopft Doubleday Publishing Group, a division of Penguin Random House LLC. All rights reserved; Extract and illustrations from *Willow* by Denise Brennan-Nelson and Rosemarie Brennan. Used with the permission of Sleeping Bear Press.

Thanks to the following for permission to reproduce images:

Cover by Omar Aranda (Beehive Illustration); Inside **Unit 1** Catherine Falls Commercial/GI; Monkeybusinessimages/GI; Adam Taylor/GI; Klaus Vedfelt; SDI Productions/GI; Valeriy_G/GI; PeopleImages/GI; Robert Young/GI; Jamras Lamyai/GI; MarsBars/GI; SDI Productions/GI; Marla Aufmuth/GI;NurPhoto/GI; Tetra Images/GI; Frankix/GI; Johner Images/GI; Julian Stratenschulte/GI; Kaphoto/GI; Russell Savory/GI; Rajesh Mhatre/EyeEm/GI; **Unit 2** Steve Smith/GI; Hannah Peters/GI; Alex Trautwig/GI; Pete Saloutos/GI; Tankist276/GI; Ajaykampani/GI; The Washington Post/GI; BSR Agency/GI; CasarsaGuru/GI; Kitipong Bhalatanya /GI; Istetiana/GI; Anass Bachar/GI; Pioneer111/GI; 32Peter Cade/GI; NurPhoto/GI; Kyodo News/GI; Kritchanon Ardsamart/GI; Gualtiero Boffi/GI; Sean Locke/GI; Image Source/GI; David Madison/GI; Frantic00/GI; peepo/GI; Barry Austin/GI; **Unit 3** John Dickson/GI; Abadonian/GI; Copyright (C) Arto Hakola. All rights reserverd/GI; ImageBROKER/GI; VMJones/GI; Wolfgang Kaehler/GI; Auscape/GI; CR Courson/GI; Dr T J Martin/GI; Kristianbell/GI; Tim Hawley/GI; Peter Johnson/GI; Dougal Waters/GI; Zen Rial/GI; Rebecca R Jackrel/GI; Spondylolithesis/GI; Jaimie Tuchman/GI; Klaus-Werner Friedrich/GI; Putra Kurniawan/GI; Atosf/GI; Abadonian/GI; lissart/GI; George Karbus Photography/GI; CathyKeifer/GI; Chase Dekker Wild-Life Images/GI; Arvind Balaraman/GI; Rebecca R Jackrel/GI; BrandyTaylor/GI; Alan Tunnicliffe Photography/GI; Paul Souders/GI; Edwin Remsberg/GI; CathyKeifer/GI; Klaus-Werner Friedrich/GI; KeithSzafranski/GI; Delta Images/GI; NurPhoto/GI; Istetiana/GI; Steve Smith/GI; Jaimie Tuchman/GI; Kristianbell/GI; **Unit 4** Xefstock/GI; lvcandy/GI; Scanrail/GI; Albln/GI; Westend61/GI; Kerkez/GI; LSOphoto/GI; Scanrail/GI; PC Format Magazine/GI; Yamaguchi Haruyoshi/GI; YOSHIKAZU TSUNO/GI; Pacific Press/GI; Michael Wapp/GI; John B. Carnett/GI; Freestylephoto/GI; Enter89/GI; Thekoala/GI; thekoala/iStockphoto/Thinkstock; 69Adastra/GI; Spooh/GI; Abid Katib/GI; Seksan Mongkhonkhamsao/GI; Sankei/GI; LSOphoto/GI; **Unit 5** Francesco Carta fotografo/GI; Richard Sharrocks/GI; LdF/GI; Bhubeth Bhajanavorakul/GI; Steven Puetzer/GI; Peter Dazeley/GI; Andresr/GI; Pollyana Ventura/GI; Tek Image/Science Photo Library/GI; Kroach/GI; Rbozuk/GI; Kali9/GI; Brittany Murray/MediaNews Group/Long Beach Press-Telegram/GI; Subir Halder/The India Today Group/GI; Diane Labombarbe/GI; Richard Sharrocks/GI; Cindy Ord/GI; Chesnot/GI; Photography taken by Mario Gutiérrez/GI; Peter Cade/GI; Betsie Van der Meer/GI; Xavier Bonghi/GI; **Unit 6** Georgijevic/GI; Kali9/GI; Westend61/GI; Stephen Simpson Inc/GI; Maskot/GI; Rich Carey / Shutterstock; Andresr/GI; Serts/GI; Fuse/GI; Kiattisak Lamchan/GI; Klaus Vedfelt/GI; Westend61/GI; Tom Grubbe/GI; NASA/Bryan Allen/GI; Kali9/GI; Peter Dazeley/GI; Serts/GI; Kiattisak Lamchan/GI; Richard Sharrocks/GI; Erik Simonsen/GI;
Unit 7 Lysogor/GI; Richard Roscoe/Stocktrek Images/GI; Joseph Johnson/GI; Andrew Steele/GI; Salvatore Virzi/GI; Tom Pfeiffer/VolcanoDiscovery/GI; Justinreznick/GI; Mike Korostelev/GI; Boris Jordan Photography/GI; imageBROKER/Robert Seitz/GI; Kazuhiro Nogi/GI; Hepatus/Gi; Willoughby Owen/GI; Antonio Busiello/GI; Jenifoto/GI; Carlo Hermann,Carlo Hermann/GI; DeAgostini/GI; Ulimi/GI; Juan Sebastian Cuellar Rodriguez/GI; JordiStock/GI; Warren Faidley/GI; Ingólfur Bjargmundsson/GI; Justinreznick/GI; Salvatore Virzi/GI; Boris Jordan Photography/GI; **Unit 8** Subbotina Anna/Shutterstock; Nick David/GI; Adventtr/GI; Et-Artworks/GI; Isabel Pavia/GI; BFA/Alamy Stock Photo; Dhemmy Zeirifandi/GI; Ben Molyneux/Alamy Stock Photo; Pagadesign/GI; Westend61/GI; DmitryMo/GI; Valentinrussanov/GI; Maskot/GI; t_kimura/GI; Universal Pictures/GI; Universal Pictures/GI; Thomas Demarczyk/GI; Vlatko Gasparic/GI; BFA/Alamy Stock Photo; Pagadesign/GI; DmitryMo/GI; **Unit 9** NurPhoto/GI; Miguel Navarro/GI; Pol Albarrán/GI; Aluxum/GI; Richard Levine/Corbis via Getty Images; Education Images/GI; Henryk Sadura/GI; Russell Monk/GI; NurPhoto/GI; Norberto Duarte/GI; NurPhoto/GI; NurPhoto/GI; Mint Images/GI; Mike Kemp/GI; Davit85/GI; Sviatlana Lazarenka/GI; Andrea Pistolesi/GI; Allan Baxter/GI; Salvator Barki/GI; Zetter/GI; Mark Williamson/GI; Manfred Gottschalk/GI; MasterLu/GI; Westend61/GI; Stephen Simpson Inc/GI; Karla Aquino/GI; Jasper Cole/GI

GI = Getty Images

1 ▶ My world

We are going to...

- **talk** about feelings that connect us
- **discover** how to find locations on a world map
- **talk** about someone who we admire
- **describe** our feelings about a first-time experience
- **read** about a girl with an unusual name.

Getting started

What makes us who we are?

a   What activities and events can you see in the photos?
    What activities and events are part of your world?

b   What do you think 'identity' is? What makes up your identity?

c   What do you have in common with the people around you?
    What things are different?

 Watch this!

1.1 What connects us to others?

We are going to...

- talk about feelings that connect us.

1 **Think:** How do the photos make you feel? Match each photo to an emotion. Then make connections with your own experiences. Compare your ideas with your partner.

happy   nervous   angry   scared   excited   interested

I've got a cat. She makes me feel happy when I'm with her.

01 2 **Listen:** Which pictures do the children talk about? Which emotions do they match with the images? Are they the same or different to your ideas?

3 **Talk:** What ideas do the children have in common? Which ones are different?

They both get angry when...   *The cat makes the boy... because...*

4 **Listen** to the children's teacher describe the Connections game. How do you play the game? What is its purpose?

 5 **Use of English:** Two students are discussing their words. Complete their questions from the conversation. How did the children answer? Write two ideas they have in common.

a _____ you finished yet?

b Why have you _____ a football?

c Why _____ you _____ 'mean'?

6 **Vocabulary:** Look at these words from the children's conversations. Work with your partner. Which words are positive and which are negative? How do you know?

> win   bully   scratch   awesome   cool
> mean   harm   pollution   starve

Use of English – Present perfect

We use the present perfect tense to describe events in the recent past, when the time of the event is not important.

I have drawn a car...

7 **Talk: Play the Connections game!**

- Take a piece of paper and divide it into six parts. Think about the emotions in Activity 1.
- Draw something or write a word in each part which makes you feel one of the emotions.
- Now compare your ideas with your partner and find connections!
- Share your connections with your class.

Why have you written...?

Because I feel excited when...

We both feel happy when...

The Connections Game!

❯ 1.2 Where in the world am I?

Me
31 New Street
Fenton
York
North Yorkshire
UK
Europe
Planet Earth

We are going to...

• discover how to find locations on a world map.

1 **Talk:** Where is your place in the world? Match the words to the lines of the address. Then match them to your own address.

> town/city   country   street   county/province   district   continent

2 Which parts of your address are *local, national, international* and *global*?

04 3 **Read:** How do you **pinpoint** exact locations on a world map? Read and listen to the text. Label the Earth diagram on page 15.

4 Read the text again and look at the world cities on the map on page 15. Match each city to a coordinate, a–d. Which countries are the cities in?

　a 13° N 100° E   b 33° S 151° E   c 41° N 29° E   d 23° S 43° W

5 Read the Use of English box. Find other examples of prepositions before nouns in the text.

6 Work in small groups. Find your town or city on the world map. Find the nearest lines of latitude and longitude.

• Research: find three interesting places with the same latitude and three places with the same longitude. Look for...

> cities   famous buildings
> mountain ranges   volcanoes

**Use of English –
Prepositions before nouns**

Prepositions give us more information about the nouns in a sentence, for example where something is.

... places **on** our planet
... parallel **to** the equator

• Write the coordinate for each place and some interesting information. Use prepositional phrases in your sentences.

... is one of the hottest places **on our planet***...*

• Present your findings to your class. Give your classmates the coordinates to find the places on the map, then tell them something interesting about each place.

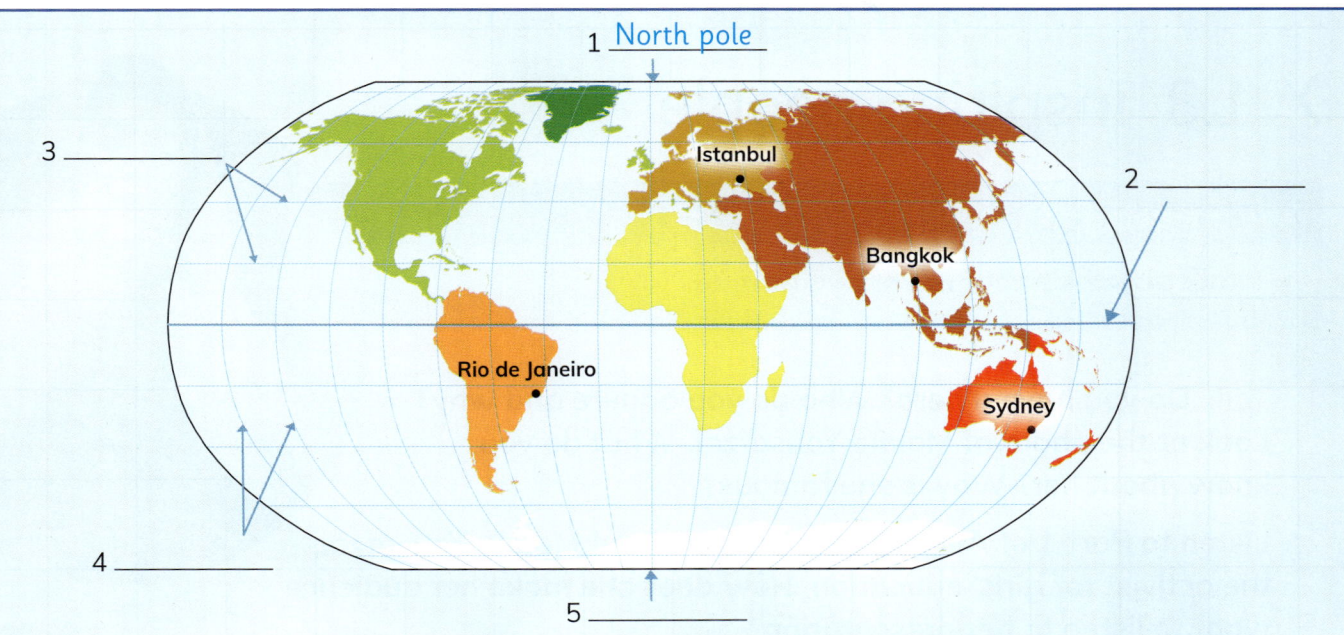

1 North pole

2 _____

3 _____

4 _____

5 _____

Istanbul

Bangkok

Rio de Janeiro

Sydney

Planet Earth is huge, so how do we pinpoint the exact location of places on our planet?

We map the Earth's surface with lines called **latitude** and **longitude**. Imagine our planet as a huge ball or sphere. At one end is the **North Pole** and at the other, the **South Pole**. In the middle, circling the Earth between the two poles, is an imaginary line called the **equator**. Its line of latitude is zero **degrees** (0°). More lines of latitude circle the Earth from east to west, **parallel** to the equator. They are the same distance apart (about 111 km); each distance is measured in degrees, 0–90° to the north and 0–90° to the south.

Lines of longitude run from the North Pole to the South Pole. The lines divide the Earth's surface into **vertical** sections, like pieces of an orange. These lines are measured in degrees too, 0–180° to the east and 0–180° to the west.

What happens when a location is between the lines? We divide the degrees into minutes and seconds, so the exact location can be found. This code is called a **coordinate**.

Remember that these are imaginary lines – you can't actually see them!

Key words: map reading

pinpoint: to find out or say the exact position

pole: the most northern and southern points of the Earth

degree: a unit of measurement

parallel: two lines of equal distance apart

vertical: standing upwards

coordinate: a code with numbers and letters that shows exact positions on a map

> 1.3 Inspiring people

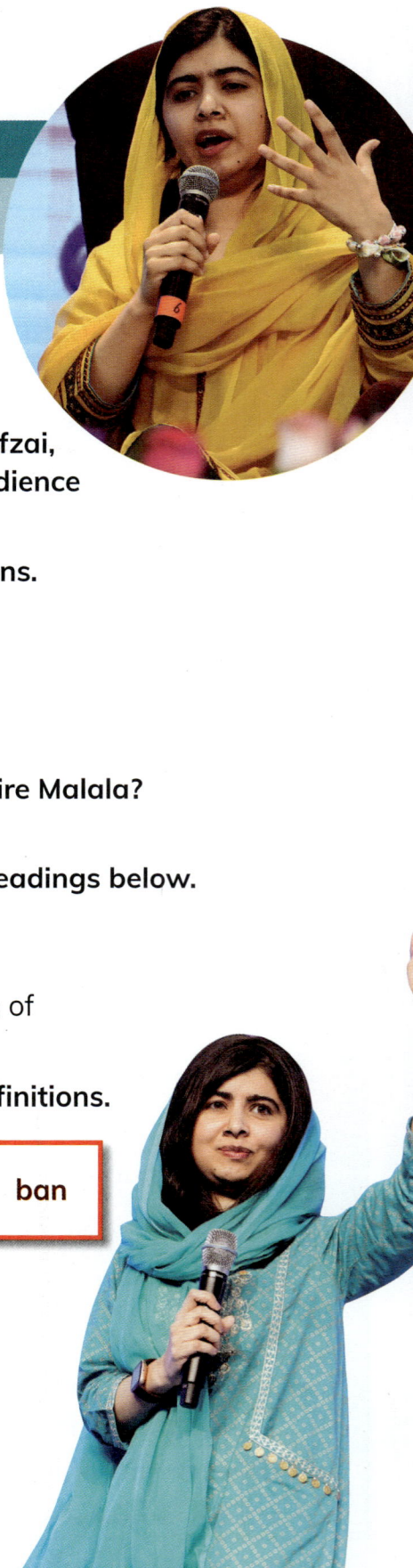

We are going to...

- **talk about someone who we admire.**

1 **Talk:** Do you have a hero? Who do you admire and why? Look at the photo of Malala Yousafzai. What do you know about her? Why is she famous?

 2 **Listen** to Part 1 of Aliya's presentation about Malala Yousafzai, the activist for girls' education. How does she make her audience want to listen to her presentation?

 3 **Listen** to Part 2 of Aliya's presentation. Answer the questions.

   a Who thought school was important for girls?
   b What did Malala do when her school was closed?
   c What happened when Malala was 15 years old? Why?
   d How did Malala react to this event?

 4 **Listen** to Part 3 of Aliya's presentation. Why does she admire Malala? How does she finish her presentation?

 5 **Listen** to Parts 1–3 again. Match the three parts with the headings below.

   a Malala's early life, her work and why she is famous.
   b Why Aliya chose to talk about Malala.
   c The purpose of the presentation and getting the attention of the audience.

6 **Vocabulary:** Match words from the presentation to their definitions.

admire	media	protest	activist	campaign	ban

   a A person who takes action to support their beliefs.
   b To think very well of someone.
   c To refuse to allow something.
   d The internet, newspapers, TV, magazines.
   e To disagree and complain very strongly.
   f To organise activities to achieve something.

7 Pronunciation: Listen and repeat the *-tion/-sion* words from the presentation. What sound do you hear at the end of the words?

a   introduction

b   education

c   decision

d   presentation

> **Speaking tip**
>
> ### Order your presentation
>
> Use sequencing words to help your audience follow your presentation.
>
> Today, I'm going to talk about…
>
> As I said in my introduction, she is a…
>
> By this time, she was…
>
> Since then, with her father, she…
>
> To sum up, I chose to…

8 Word study: Read the speaking tip box. Which phrases are used:

a   at the beginning

b   in the middle

c   at the end of the presentation?

9 Present it! Prepare a presentation about someone you admire. Use what you have learned from Aliya's presentation to help you.

- Research interesting facts about your subject and make notes. Use the internet or the library.
- Organise your notes into sections. Use the headings in Activity 5 to help you.
- Add sequencing words and think of a way to get the attention of your audience at the beginning. For example, with a question, an interesting fact or a picture.
- Does your presentation need any props? For example, pictures, videos or real objects.
- Practise your presentation with a partner.
- Perform your presentation in front of your class. Listen to your classmates' presentations and write a question to ask at the end. Write down one interesting fact from each one.

> 1.4 A first time for everything

We are going to...

- describe our feelings about a first-time experience.

1 **Talk:** Have you done anything recently you have never done before? How did the experience make you feel?

2 **Read:** These children are describing a first-time experience. Find key words to describe what each child did, why it was special and their feelings about the experience.

1 **Olivia, 11** It doesn't seem so amazing now but I remember the first time I saw the sea on a school trip. I looked at it in amazement. It was so beautiful and so huge! I asked my teacher, 'How big is it?' and **he gave me a funny smile** and explained that it was very big! We **live** in a city far from the coast and **I've only ever been** to the seaside twice in my life.

verb + objects

present simple

present perfect for experiences

verb + object + infinitive

2 **Santok, 11** Last year, I went on a rollercoaster for the first time. **My friend asked me to go with him** and I was really scared; but I decided to push myself and try it. It was **exciting** and **terrifying** at the same time! It climbed up and up and then suddenly dropped down really fast. That bit was the worst – I closed my eyes and screamed! It was okay because everyone else was screaming too, so that made me feel better. When it was finished, I felt a sense of pride for doing something brave. But I haven't been on a rollercoaster again!

powerful adjectives

past simple

3 **Cody, 12** I **felt** really proud of myself when I first learned to swim! My dad taught me to swim and I remember that feeling of excitement very well. I was six years old and I had a fear of water. I didn't want to go in the water. But when I learned how to swim I wasn't afraid of it any more. I felt very satisfied because I had achieved something big. Since then, I have never been afraid of water again.

3 Word study: Copy and complete the table with adjectives and nouns from the descriptions. Then talk about an experience or feeling you've had using these words.

Nouns	Adjectives
a	amazing
amazement	
beauty	b
terror	c
d	proud
bravery	e
f	excited
satisfaction	g

4 Talk: Work in pairs. Match questions a–c to the children's answers in Activity 2. Then ask and answer the questions with your partner.

a   Have you ever felt really proud of yourself? What did you do?

b   Have you ever seen something you thought was amazing? What did you see?

c   Have you ever done something you were scared of? What did you do?

Language focus – Verb patterns

Some verbs are followed by other words in a specific order:

… he **gave** me a funny smile…
   verb + objects

My friend **asked** me to go with him…
   verb + object + infinitive (with to)

The **object** is the person/thing affected by the verb action.

Writing tip

Using key words

Make a note of key words before you start writing. Then use the key words to build your sentences.

5 Use of English: Read Cody's description again. Can you find another example of the verb pattern, verb + object + infinitive (with *to*)?

6 Write a description of a first-time experience.

Step 1: Make notes and plan	• Read the Writing tip box. Write key words to describe a special experience. Think of nouns, verbs and adjectives. Use the table in Activity 3 to help you. • Use questions to plan your description. Build sentences using your key words. What did you do? Why was it special? How did it make you feel? Why?
Step 2: Writing	• Use your answers to the questions to organise your description. • Use different verb tenses. • Use adjectives and nouns to describe your feelings.
Step 3: Read and check	Swap with a partner. Find similarities and differences in your descriptions. Then proofread each other's work and circle any errors. Correct the errors and ask your teacher to check.

> 1.5 A Girl Called Owl

We are going to...

- read about a girl with an unusual name.

1 **Talk:** What do you think about your name? Does it have a special meaning? Is there any special reason why you are called your name?

2 **Read and listen** to Parts 1 and 2 of the story. What is the girl's name? What does her name mean? Then read again. Are the sentences that follow each section true or false?

A Girl Called Owl
by Amy Wilson

Part 1

When you have a kid, don't call it something stupid.

Don't call it Apple or Pear or Mung Bean.

Don't call it Owl.

This advice is a bit late for me. Because she did. She did call me Owl. Thirteen years ago she looked down at a tiny little baby – me – and decided that Owl would be a good way to go.

I guess she didn't know then that I would have white-blond hair that flicks around my face, like **feathers**, no matter what I do with it. That my eyes would turn from baby blue to the palest brown, almost yellow; that my nose would be on the **beaky** side.

She should have seen that last one coming though; I **inherited** it from her.

I like owls. I think they're beautiful, but you know, my head doesn't **rotate** 360 degrees. I can't fly. I don't hunt at night.

All these are questions the other kids have asked me, over the years. Mum laughs when I tell her.

'See!' she cries, looking up from whatever she's doing, a glint in her dark eyes. 'Already you stand out in the crowd. Already you are different. Isn't it a wonderful thing?'

She's beautiful, my mum. Not in a **subjective** way, like she's my mum therefore she must be beautiful. She's actually beautiful. She has these big dark eyes, **masses** of dark hair, and when she smiles, when she laughs, it's difficult not to join in.

I do try my very best not to join in.

Her name is Isolde. She wears lots of bright colours, and **tinkling bangles** on her wrists. She smells of warm things: **vanilla**, cinnamon, oranges and blackcurrants, and something deeper that's just her, I guess.

My friends love her.

Which is annoying.

a	Owl likes her unusual name.	true / false
b	Owl thinks that she looks like an owl in some ways.	true / false
c	She doesn't look like her mum at all.	true / false
d	Other children have asked questions about her name.	true / false
e	Owl's mum thinks the other children's questions are a good thing.	true / false
f	Owl is pleased that her friends like her mum.	true / false

Glossary

beaky: shaped like a bird's beak

subjective: influenced by personal feelings (not facts)

tinkling: a sound like a bell

bangles: a type of jewellery for your wrist

vanilla: a substance used to add taste to sweet foods

Part 2

Owl and her friend, Mallory, have just had a maths lesson.
Owl was told off by the teacher for sketching owls instead of paying attention.

It was an owl. The doodle in my maths book. I draw them, over and over. Little ones, big ones, owls with crazy **whirly** eyes, owls **swooping** down from the sky. They're in all the **borders** of my lined school books. They're on Post-it notes around my bedroom. I have **sketches** of them, paintings, even little clay figures.

I'm not saying they're good. Actually, if you walked into my bedroom, you'd probably run back out again, screaming. They're a bit **intense**.

Mum loves them. *Loves* them. She thinks it's me expressing myself.

Drawing myself, over and over again.

Mallory just rolls her eyes when she sees a new one now. She bought me a card with a **puffin** on it for my birthday a couple of weeks ago.

'Maybe a change?' she wrote inside, 'Now that you're thirteen?'

But I'm not *called* Puffin.

And there had to be a reason.

A reason Mum called me Owl.

g	Owl draws lots of pictures of owls in her school books and in her bedroom.	true / false
h	Her mum doesn't like her drawings.	true / false
i	Her friend Mallory thinks she should continue drawing lots of owls.	true / false
j	Owl thinks that there must be an explanation for her unusual name.	true / false

Glossary

borders: edges
sketches: simple drawings
puffin: a type of sea bird

3   Work in pairs. Can you correct the false sentences?

4   Answer the questions. Find sentences in the story to support your answers to the inference questions.

   a   How do you think Owl feels about the questions other children ask her?

   b   Do you think Owl is always happy with her mum?

   c   Why does Owl think her drawings are 'a bit intense'?

   d   Why do you think she is always drawing pictures of owls?

> **Reading tip**
>
> **Inference**
>
> The answers to inference questions are not in the story text. To answer, you must use clues in the text, and your own experience, then draw a conclusion.

5   **Word study:** Work out the meaning of the words in blue in the story by looking at other words in the sentence. Then match to the definitions.

   a   to fly down very fast

   b   something that covers a bird's body

   c   to be born with the same features as one of your parents

   d   a pattern of circles

   e   lots of

   f   very strong feeling

   g   move round and round

6   **Talk** about the questions in groups.

   a   Which features and characteristics have you inherited from members of your family?

     I have dark eyes like my dad...

   b   Why do you think Owl's mum chose her name for her? Do you know anyone with an unusual name? How do they feel about it?

7   **Values:** Accepting our differences. Owl's mum is pleased that her name makes her 'stand out from the crowd', but Owl is not so sure. What advice would you give her?

> Your name is special because it is unique, you should be proud of it.

8   In what ways can we feel different to other people? How can this be a good thing?

〉 1.6 Project challenge

Project A: A presentation about something or someone special to you

1 Prepare a presentation about one of these topics.
Work individually or find a classmate with a similar idea.
Use your presentation on page 17 to help you.

- An interesting or special experience you've had.
- Your favourite free-time activity.

2 Decide which topic to present and make notes.
Use the internet or library resources to help you.

3 Plan your presentation using these guidelines.

- Give the purpose of the presentation and something to attract the audience's attention at the beginning.
- Explain the background to the subject.
- Explain what is special or interesting about the subject.
- Give a short summary to finish the presentation.

4 Add photos, music, videos or any other props.

5 Deliver your presentation. If you are working with a classmate, divide the tasks of the presentation equally. Who is going to introduce the presentation? Who is going to organise the props?

Project B: Design an 'Our names' poster for your classroom

1 Work in a group of four. Choose one of these options.

 A Use the internet or library resources to research the history of your first name. Find out how old your name is and if it has a special meaning.

Ying Yue

My name means 'reflection of the moon'...

 OR

 B Find out the top five most popular names for boys or girls in your country. Research the history of those names.

2 Write a paragraph about the names you have chosen. If you chose Option A, add information about why your parents chose your name for you.

3 Create a large group poster:

 • Make a large colourful heading for each first name or the top five names.
 • Add the information you have found out about your name(s).
 • Decorate the poster with images connected to your name(s).

4 Present your poster to your class.

 • Deliver your presentation as a group with each classmate taking a turn to present their name or the top five names.
 • Explain the information on the poster and why you have chosen the visual images for each name.

5 Display your posters on the wall of your classroom.

What did you enjoy most about doing your project?

› 1.7 What do you know now?

What makes us who we are?

1. Write a sentence about something that makes you…
**happy   angry   excited
nervous   interested   scared**

2. Write five sentences about things you (or your family and friends) have done recently.
**I have done a project about…
I have learned to…**

3. How would you explain **latitude** and **longitude** to a younger child? Practise with your partner.

4. Write the noun forms of these adjectives.
**amazing   exciting
terrifying   beautiful
satisfied   proud**

5. Why did Aliya choose to talk about Malala on page 16?

6. How do Owl's features reflect her name in the story on pages 20–22?

Look what I can do!

Write or show examples in your notebook.	😐	🙂
I can talk about feelings and compare with my friends.	○	○
I can use the present perfect to talk about things that happened recently.	○	○
I can find locations on a map using coordinates.	○	○
I can use prepositional phrases to build sentences.	○	○
I can do a presentation about someone I admire.	○	○
I can describe a first-time experience.	○	○
I can read and understand a story about a girl with an unusual name.	○	○

2 ▶ Sport

We are going to...

- **talk** about different types of sport
- **find out** how food helps us to do sport
- **give** instructions for sports exercises using modal verbs
- **write** a biography about a sports star
- **read** and **enjoy** a story about a football match.

Getting started

What can we learn from doing and watching sports?

a   Do you do any of the sports in the photos? What kind of equipment can you see?

b   Think about your favourite sport or physical activity. What skills do you need? How do you learn and practise those skills?

c   Look at the photos. What are the benefits of sport?

 Watch this!

> 2.1 What can we get from sport?

We are going to...

- talk about different types of sport.

1 Talk: Which sports do you do? Why? Where and when do you do sport?

a

b

c

d

e

f

2 Vocabulary: Match a photo in Activity 1 with the words in the box.

> football   judo   gymnastics   tennis   basketball   swimming
> badminton   volleyball   athletics   hockey

3 Listen: Which sports in the box are the children talking about?

4 Listen again and decide if these sentences are true or false. Correct the false sentences.

   a Speaker 1 loves his sport because he can play it in lots of different places.

   b Speaker 2 likes being in a team because they always win.

   c Speaker 3 often feels good after doing his sport.

   d Speaker 4 likes her sport because she can play it in a big team.

5 Talk about the reasons why the children like their sports. What other reasons are there?

6 Vocabulary: Match the pictures to words in the box.
Then match the equipment to the sports in Activity 2.

shuttlecock   belt   goalposts   net
shin pads   racquet   hockey stick   goggles

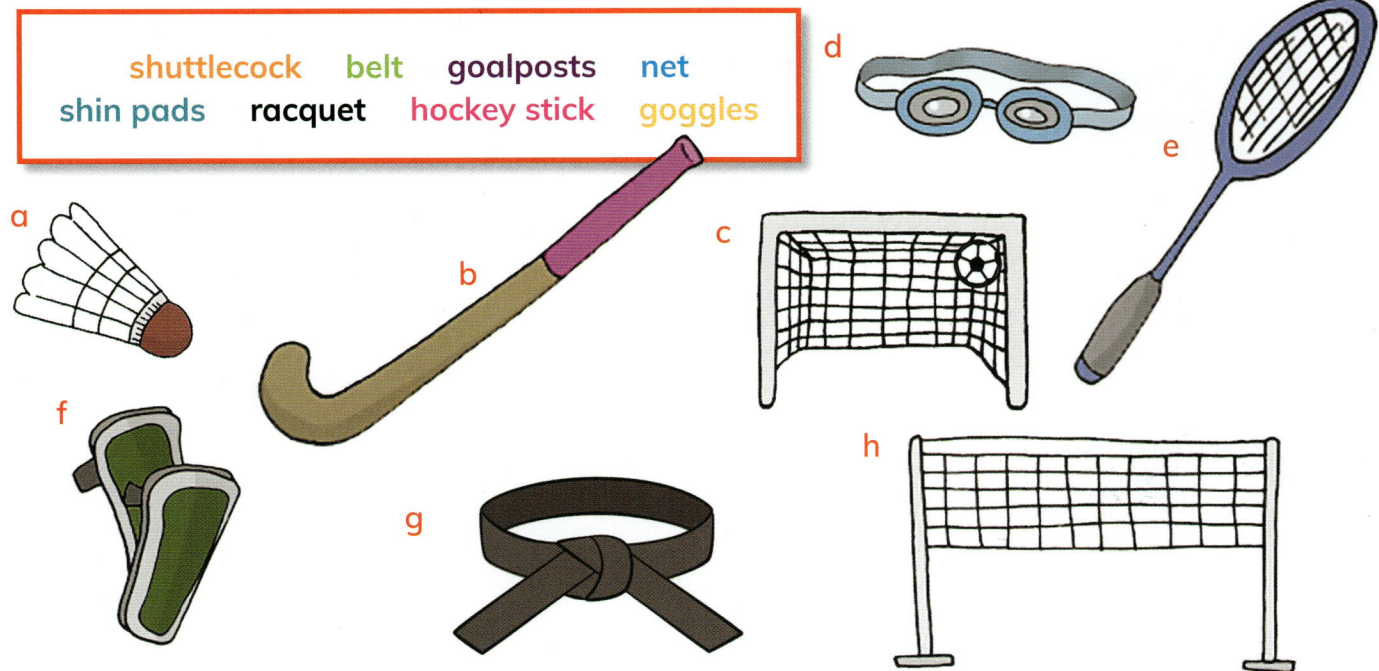

7 Talk: What equipment do we need for the sports?
Talk to your partner.

You need a shuttlecock to play badminton.

8 What about you? Ask and answer in pairs.

a   What sport do you like best?
b   What is the best thing about your favourite sport?
c   What equipment do you need for your favourite sport?

9 Look at Shireen's bar chart. Which question in Activity 8 did she ask her classmates?

10 Write: Choose a question in Activity 8 and ask a group of your classmates. Make notes about their answers and draw a bar chart to show the results.

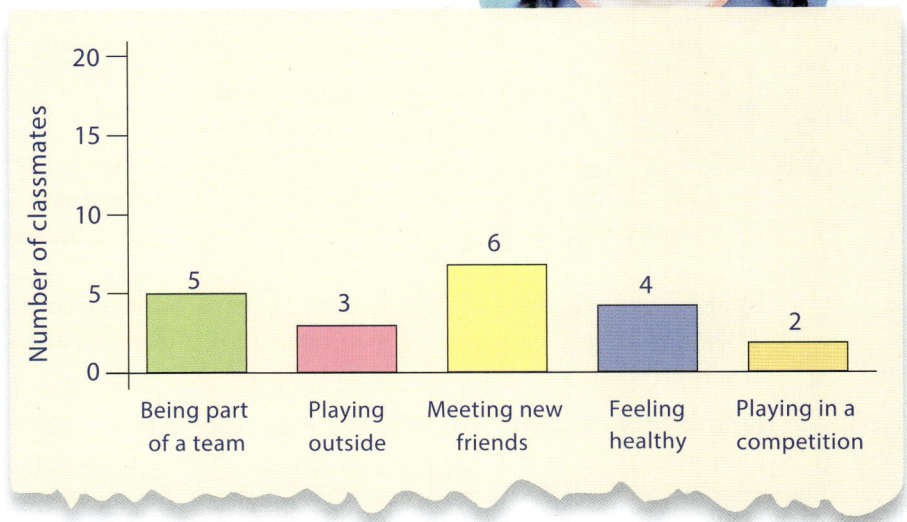

› 2.2 Eat for strength and energy!

We are going to...

- find out how food helps us to do sport.

Reading tip

Finding specific information

First, decide what information you want to find out in a text. Then look for that information when you read.

1   **Talk: What do you know about food and exercise? What kind of food helps you with sports and physical activity?**

2   **Improve your energy! Find out how with a quick quiz! Are the statements true or false?**

a	Yoghurt and milk help to build strong bones.	true / false
b	If you eat sugary food, you'll have energy for a long time.	true / false
c	Make sure you have lots to eat before doing exercise.	true / false
d	If you drink plenty of water, it'll stop you from feeling thirsty.	true / false

 3   **Read and listen to the text and check your answers to the quiz in Activity 2.**

Tips for health and energy!

Did you know that top athletes pay as much attention to what they eat as how they train? Your eating habits can really help your body when you do sports and exercise. Here's how to keep your body in tip-top condition.

Eat healthy carbohydrates like wholemeal bread, pasta, brown rice, vegetables and beans. You will give your body energy for exercise and feel fuller for longer.

Don't eat too much white bread and sugary food. If you eat these foods, you'll get a quick energy lift, but later you'll feel tired more quickly.

Eat protein to help your body get stronger. Protein repairs your muscles after exercise and helps your blood cells carry **nutrients** and **oxygen** to your muscles. Good protein foods are chicken, fish, eggs, milk, green vegetables and lentils.

Drink plenty of milk and eat yoghurt. These foods contain calcium to give you strong bones.

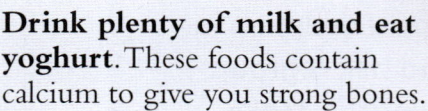

Feel hungry before doing sport? Have a banana or some other fruit! This food is easy to **digest**. If you have a lot of food before exercise, you'll probably get a stomach ache!

Drink lots of water. Your body needs water to stay healthy. If you drink plenty of water, you'll stay cool and hydrated when you do sport.

Key words: nutrition

carbohydrate: a substance in food that provides the body with energy

nutrients: substances you need to live and grow

oxygen: a chemical you need to live and breathe

digest: to change food so your body can use it

4 Talk: Which tips in the text do you follow already?
What other tips do you know? Talk to your partner!

5 Use of English: Read the Use of English box and match the sentence halves.

1   If you eat less sugary food,
2   If you eat foods with calcium,
3   You'll feel thirsty and tired
4   Unless you eat enough carbohydrates,
5   If you eat plenty of fruit and vegetables,

a   your bones will grow strong.
b   if you don't drink enough water.
c   you'll have more energy.
d   your body will get the vitamins it needs.
e   you won't have enough energy.

Use of English – First conditional with *if* / *unless*

We use the first conditional to express future events that are likely to happen:

if / *unless* + present simple + *will* / *won't* + verb

If you **drink** plenty of water, you**'ll stay** hydrated.
Your body **won't grow** well **unless** you get plenty of protein.

(in this sentence, *unless* = *if you don't...*)

6   Find more examples of the first conditional in the text.

7 Write: Make an energy tips poster, using first conditional sentences.
Use the information in the text and your own ideas.

Try to eat two fruit and three vegetables a day.
If you eat enough fruit and vegetables, you'll...

〉 2.3 Ready to go!

We are going to...

- give instructions for sports exercises using modal verbs.

1 **Talk:** Before you do any sports, you need to do warm-up exercises. What are warm-up exercises? What parts of the body should you warm up and how?

2 **Vocabulary:** Match the words in the box with the labels on the picture in your notebook.

ankle	shoulder	thighs	calves
hip	bottom	toes	knees	heart

3 **Listen** to Sam giving instructions for warm-up exercises. Put the pictures in order. Which parts of the body are mentioned?

a

b

c

4 Now stand up. Listen again and do the warm-up exercises. How do you feel afterwards?

Use of English – need / should / mustn't for advice and instructions

We use **need** when something is necessary:

First, we **need** to get your heart pumping...

We use **should** to give advice:

You **should** warm up your hips too...

We use **mustn't** to give strong advice against something:

You **mustn't** start running without warming up your leg muscles.

 5 **Use of English:** Listen to the last warm-up exercise again.
Complete the advice and instructions.

⚡ Warm-up advice ⚡

a   You _____ warm up your upper body.

b   Your arms _____ be straight.

c   You _____ do about 15 turns.

d   You _____ rotate them too fast or you'll hurt your muscles.

6   **Talk:** Do you know any other warm-up exercises?
Make notes of instructions you want to give.
Tell your partner what to do. Which part of the body do they exercise?
Use the pictures below to help you.

First, you should...

> ## 2.4 Our favourite sports stars

We are going to...

- write a biography about a sports star.

1 **Talk:** Who are your favourite sports stars? Why? What do you know about their lives?

2 **Read** the biography of Simone Biles, the world-famous gymnast. How many gold medals has she won?

High flyer!

present perfect

A Simone Biles is the most successful gymnast of all time. She **has won** more World Championship medals than any other man or woman in the history of gymnastics. Simone was one of the superstars at the Olympic Games in Rio, where, at just 19 years old, she won four gold and one bronze medals. She said at the time, **'My first Olympics and I've walked away with five medals… It shows dreams can come true. I'm not the next Usain Bolt or Michael Phelps: I'm the first Simone Biles.'**

quote

dates

B Simone was born in Ohio, USA in **1997**. When she was very young, she was in foster care until she and her younger sister, Adria, were adopted by their grandparents. She was always a very active child, who loved jumping around. Then her life changed at the age of six, on a school trip to a gymnastics centre. There, a coach noticed her natural talent and invited her to join a class.

C From that moment, with the support of her family, Simone **worked** hard to become an excellent gymnast. She was very small, but strong. In third grade, she was teased by her classmates about her muscly legs. Instead of getting upset, she felt proud because she knew she was stronger than most of the other children!

past simple

D Simone has had setbacks in her journey to stardom, but she **has never given up.** In 2011, she just missed being selected for the National team. She was devastated, but she stayed strong and positive and used the experience to improve. Three years later her determination was rewarded: in 2014, she became the first woman in 40 years to win **four** gold medals at the World Championships!

present perfect

numbers

3 **Read the text again and match the headings 1–4 to the paragraphs A–D.**

1 Simone's early life.
2 Present-day success.
3 Her journey to stardom.
4 Some information about her childhood.

4 **Word study: Find these words in the biography. What do they mean? Discuss with your partner.**

> talent   give up   foster care   improve
> coach   tease

Reading tip

Focus on dates and numbers

Use dates and numbers to find important information in a text.

5 **Read the Reading tip box. Why are these dates and numbers important to Simone's story?**

a five
b third grade
c 2011
d 2014

6 **Talk to your partner about Simone's story and answer the questions.**

a Read the Writing tip box and find an example of a **quote**. What does the quote tell you about the way Simone sees her success?
b For you, what is the most interesting or surprising fact about Simone's life?

Writing tip

Use quotes

When you write about a famous person, use **quotes** to give the reader an idea of the person's personality. Quotes can come from the person or someone who knows them.

7 **Write a biography about an interesting sports person.**

Step 1: Research	Find information about your sports person on the internet or in magazines. Use the headings (1–4) in Activity 3 to help you find key information. Remember to look for important dates and numbers. Find an interesting quote.
Step 2: Planning	Use the headings to plan your biography. Plan your paragraphs in the same order.
Step 3: Writing	• Use the headings, dates and numbers to build your biography. • Use the past simple and present perfect. • Include an interesting quote.
Step 4: Read and check	Swap with a partner. Check for any errors.

〉 2.5 An extract from Off Side

We are going to...

- read and enjoy a story about a football match.

1 **Talk:** Have you ever been to a live sports event? What was it like? How did you feel?

 2 **Read and listen** to Part 1. Danny and his dad are at a live game. How does Danny help his dad? Why does he need to do this?

 3 **Read and listen** to Part 1 again and answer the questions at the end.

Off Side by Tom Palmer

1 Danny and his dad came to every City home game. And Danny acted as commentator because, when he was younger, his dad had been blinded in an accident. He'd had to stop work, stop playing **football** with Danny, stop almost everything.

Danny remembered worrying if his dad would give up *going* to the football too, but on the day of the first game, after he was out of hospital, dad had stood up.

'Danny?'

'Yeah.'

'Come on, son. City are at home. What are you waiting for?'

Since then, Danny had become skilled at describing live football, telling his dad just enough so that he could follow the game…

a What is the name of Danny's football team?
b Do Danny and his dad watch them in their home city or away?

 4 **Read and listen** to the description of the live football match. Choose the correct answer to the questions after each section.

2 … The second half was fantastic. City poured players forward. Their **twin strike force** looked lethal. Sam Roberts, England's leading scorer and new sensation, Ghanaian international Anthony Owusu. Danny struggled to keep up his commentary just as much as the United defenders **struggled** to keep up with City's strikers.

'Owusu is playing deep,' Danny told his dad. 'Roberts further up.'

And as he spoke, City's **midfield dynamo launched** a high cross into the United area. The ball ricocheted off a defender to Owusu, who controlled it on his knee and **volleyed** it with amazing power. At first the ball seemed to be going way over, but then it began to dip into a powerful arc. Half a second later, it was crashing in off the crossbar and **bouncing** about in the goal.

a Why is City player, Sam Roberts, special?
    1 He's scored a lot of goals.
    2 He is captain of the England team.

b Where is Anthony Owusu from?
    1 South America   **2** Africa

c Danny finds it difficult to describe the game because…
    1 it is so exciting that he can't describe everything.
    2 his dad can't hear him.

d Owusu…
    1 misses the goal.   **2** scores a goal.

Glossary

twin strike force: two strikers who play together
midfield dynamo: the player who controls the team
launch: kick high
volley: kick the ball before it lands

3 One-nil. An **awesome** strike.

Danny and his dad leapt into each other's arms as the crowd **exploded**. First with the loudest cheer of the season, then with the name of the scorer. Over and over again.

Ow-usu! Ow-usu! Ow-usu!

When the fans had gone quiet enough for anyone to talk, Dad spoke.

'What happened?'

This always amused Danny. His dad would be leaping around, punching the air, screaming at the top of his voice one minute, then calmly asking to know why he's been jumping around in the first place.

'Owusu…' Danny said breathlessly.

'I gathered that.'

'… he just **blasted** it in!'

'Yeah?'

e   The City fans are...
    1 quite happy.   2 very happy and excited.

f   Danny's dad...
    1 understands what has happened in the game.
    2 needs Danny to explain again.

4 Danny knew his dad needed more. So he decided to give it to him: like a proper reporter on the radio. He breathed in and began.

'City's amazing Ghanaian international has scored the goal of the season. Picking the ball up on the edge of the area, he took it on his knee, then **fired** an unstoppable volley past the **paralysed** United keeper. That's Owusu's twentieth goal of the season. And just goes to show that he deserved the African Player of the Year award he received only two weeks ago.'

g   Why does Danny describe the goal like a radio reporter?
    1 To make it more exciting for his dad.
    2 To give his dad more information.
    3 Both reasons.

> **Glossary**
>
> **paralysed:** unable to move

5   Word study: Football.
Use the words in the box to label the diagram.

> strikers   defenders   (goal) keeper   midfield   goal (area)

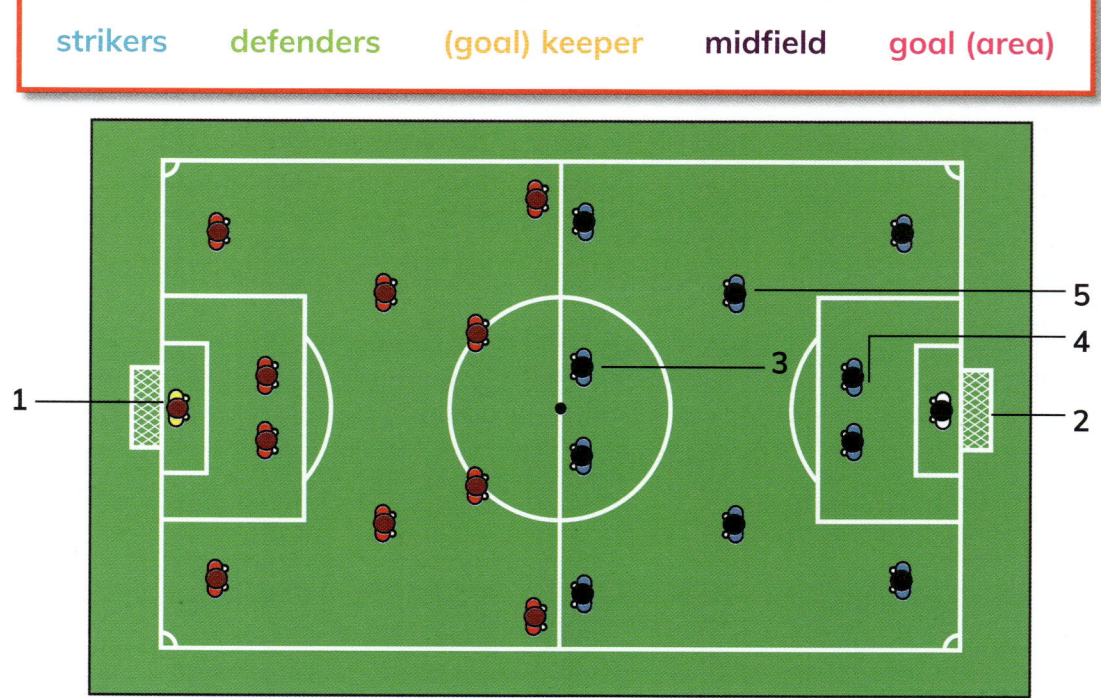

6 Word study: Descriptive words.
Look at the words in blue in the story. Try to guess any unknown words by looking at the other words and sentences in the section.

7 Replace the underlined words in the text with words from the box.

struggled   bounced   ~~blasted~~   awesome   fired   strike   exploded   keeper

Roberts (a) ~~ran very fast~~ blasted down the field with the ball, while the United defenders (b) found it difficult to stop him. Then he passed to Owusu, who (c) kicked the ball into the goal with an (d) very good (e) hit, past the shocked (f) person in the goal. The ball (g) moved up and down around the goal and the crowd (h) shouted very loudly. It was the loudest cheer I have ever heard at a home game.

8 Intonation: Read with expression by emphasising key words. Listen and repeat Danny's commentary at the end of the extract. Which words does he emphasise?

9 Write: Now write a similar description of someone scoring a goal, winning a race or a competition.

- Use words from the text or other descriptive words.
- Underline the words you want to emphasise and read your description to your partner like a radio presenter.

10 Values: Teamwork. Talk about these questions with your partner.

a   Are you a member of any sports teams?
    What responsibilities does each person have?
b   What other kinds of teams are there?
    When do you work in other teams?
c   Think of a team you're in.
    Which of these statements is true for your team?
    1   Everyone helps each other and works together to achieve something.
    2   I can learn new things from other people in the team.
    3   Other people in the team can learn something from me.
    4   Everyone in the team has a special job to do.
d   What other good things are there about being in a team?
    Are there any disadvantages?

> ## 2.6 Project challenge

Project A: Make a poster about a type of sport

1   In your groups, choose a sport or physical activity to write about. Brainstorm things you know already and write five questions about things you want to find out. Here are some topics to think about…

| equipment | clothing | safety | food and drink | rules |

2   Research your sport using the internet or the library.
Use the questions from Activity 1 to plan your research.
Each group member should take a question to research.

3   Plan your poster together. Decide on the five most important and interesting facts to include from your research.

4   Write a list of **dos** and **don'ts** about your sport. Use modal verbs and the first conditional. Add the list to the facts on your poster.

> You must do warm-up exercises before you…
> You should wear a…
> If you eat the right food, you'll…

5   When you are happy with the information on your poster, add some pictures.

6   As a class, display your posters on the wall. Read the other groups' posters and write down two new pieces of information that you didn't know before.

Project B: Create a description of a sports event

1   Work in small groups. Think of an important sports match, race or competition or invent one of your own.

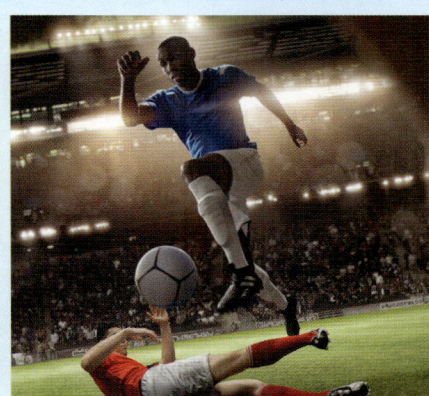

   • If it is a real event, watch it (or part of it) again on the internet, if possible.

   • Make notes about who is taking part, where it is and what happened.

2   Choose one part of the event, for example an amazing goal or someone winning a race. Write a short description.

   • Write your description in the past simple and past continuous.

   • Use descriptive words.

> … the fans were cheering!
>
> … and Luis was running down the pitch. He was so fast! Then he passed to Okoro …
>
> … and Okoro scored — what an awesome goal!

3   Ask your teacher or another group to check your first draft. Look at their comments carefully and write a second draft.

4   Now take it in turns to read the (second draft) description.

   • Read it with expression in your voice. Make your audience want to listen!

   • Listen and help each other read aloud.

5   Share your descriptions with your class. Don't say the name of the sports event – can your classmates guess what it is?

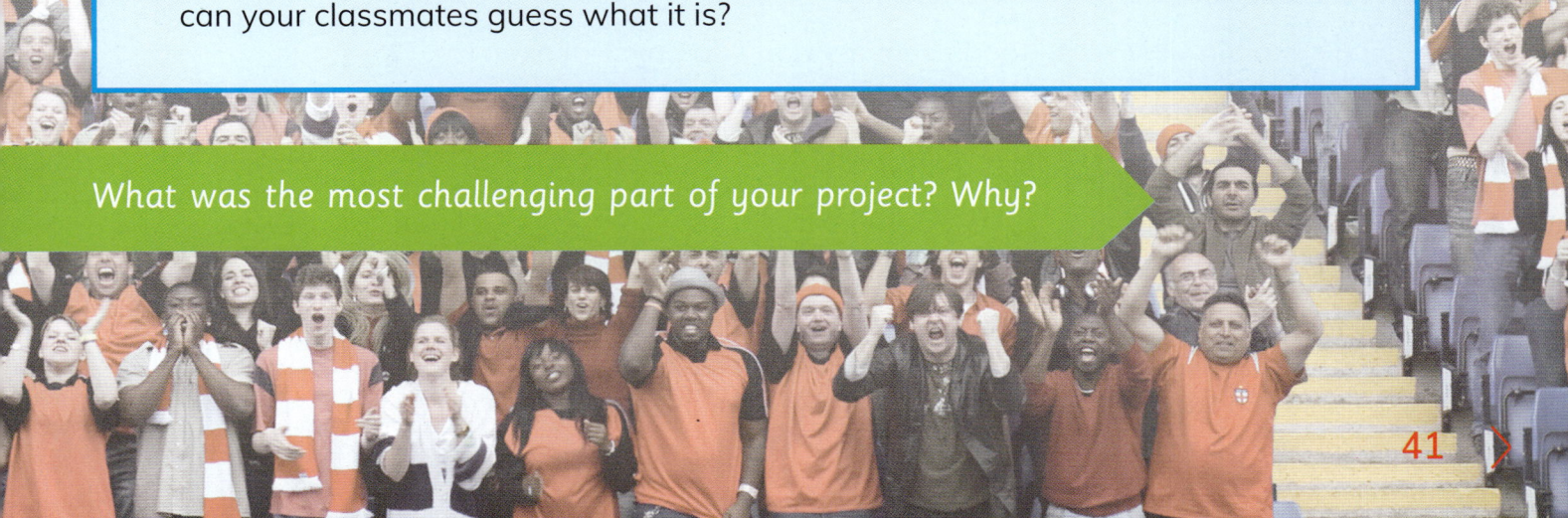

What was the most challenging part of your project? Why?

❯ 2.7 What do you know now?

What can we learn from doing and watching sports?

1 Write five pieces of sports equipment (don't show your partner). Write sentences describing how they are used. Now read the sentences to your partner. Ask them to guess the equipment.

You wear these when you go swimming. (trunks)

2 Tell your partner about your favourite sport and four things you like about it.

3 Name two food items that are good for your body when you do sport. Why are they good for you?

4 Give instructions for three warm-up exercises to your partner. They have to do the exercises. Which parts of the body are the exercises good for?

5 Write two amazing facts about Simone Biles from page 34.

6 In the football story on pages 36–38, what does Danny do to help his dad at the match? Why does he need to help him?

7 Write four good things about being in a team.

Look what I can do!

Write or show examples in your notebook.

I can talk about my favourite sports.

I can explain why some foods help my body do physical exercise.

I can use modal verbs to give instructions on how to do sports exercises.

I can write a biography about a sports star.

I can understand a story about a football match.

I can write and read out a commentary of a sports event.

3 ▶ Living things

We are going to...

- **discover** how penguins survive in the extreme cold
- **learn** how living things survive through food chains
- **present** information about animal habits using relative clauses
- **explain** key facts about carnivorous plants using *wh-* questions
- **create** an infographic text about a type of animal
- **read** a story about a connection between a girl and a whale.

Getting started

What do living things do to survive?

a   What types of living things can you see in the photos?
Match a type to a photo.

bird	mammal	amphibian	reptile	insect	fish

b   What is happening in each image?
c   How is each action helping each living thing to survive?

Watch this!

〉 3.1 Strategies for survival

We are going to...

- discover how penguins survive in the extreme cold.

1 **Talk:** What's the coldest place on Earth? How cold is it? How do you think penguin families survive there? Look at the photos for clues.

2 What do you know about emperor penguins? Work in pairs! Test yourselves with this quiz!

1 Emperor penguins live in the...

   a Arctic.   b Antarctic.

2 How long does it take them to raise their chicks?

   a Nine months   b Nine weeks

3 For protection from the cold, they keep their eggs...

   a under their wings.   b on their feet.

4 Some penguins practise looking after their eggs...

   a with a snowball.   b with a stone.

5 In the winter, for two months...

   a the sun doesn't rise.   b the sun doesn't set.

6 Which penguin protects and hatches the egg?

   a The female   b The male

7 In winter, the temperature can go down to...

   a −40°C.   b −60°C.

8 The freezing winds where they live can be...

   a 50 km per hour.   b 100 km per hour.

 3 **Listen** to Part 1 of the documentary and check your answers.

4 **Listen** to Part 2. Put the pictures in the order of the commentary.

a

b

c

d

> **Language focus –**
> **Present simple**
>
> Use the **present simple** to describe things that are always true, e.g. life cycles of animals.
>
> Mother and father penguins **work** together to feed the babies.

5 **Use of English:** Put the sentences in order, to show the development of the penguin chicks. Then match each sentence to a picture in Activity 4.

a The chicks stay balanced on their mother's feet.
b ... daylight appears again and thousands of chicks have just hatched.
c Summer arrives... The chicks are almost fully grown.
d The babies gather together for protection.

6 **Vocabulary:** Match a word from the documentary to the definitions.

> chick   breed   mate   hatch   huddle   colony

a produce young animals
b stand close together to keep warm
c a baby bird
d an animal's partner to produce young
e a group of birds that live together
f when an egg breaks and a young bird comes out

7 **Talk:** Tell your partner three new things you have learned about emperor penguins. Which facts do you think are the most interesting or surprising?

8 **Write:** What would you like to know now? Choose one of these topics and write some questions. Research the answers, then share with your class.

- Other animals in the Arctic or Antarctic.
- An animal from your country or region: find out about how it survives and protects its young.
- A tropical animal.

> 3.2 Nature's food chains

We are going to...

- learn how living things survive through food chains
- present information about animal habits using relative clauses.

1 **Talk:** Look at the photos. What do you think is the connection between these living things?

 2 **Read and listen** to the text and check your ideas for Activity 1. Answer the question at the end.

The photos show us a food chain in action. A food chain shows the relationship between living things and their sources of food. All animals and plants are important in our planet's **ecosystem** because all living things are part of food chains. Every animal on Earth depends upon a food chain for its survival.

A food chain always starts with a plant. In this process, the plant is called a **producer** because it makes its own food from the energy it gets from the sun.

The next **link** in the food chain is called a consumer and there are usually three levels. The first group are **primary consumers**: these are creatures who only eat plants. Some are called *herbivores*. Rabbits, mice and insects, such as grasshoppers are examples of herbivores. Some marine wildlife, such as krill, are also primary consumers.

The second group are **secondary consumers**: these are small animals like frogs, lizards, spiders, smaller birds and marine creatures such as squid and octopuses. They are *carnivores* whose main **diet** is meat. This group eats other animals in the primary consumer group.

Next, there are **tertiary consumers** who are usually larger animals like reptiles, birds or large fish. These animals eat the smaller creatures in the secondary consumer group.

There are also consumers whose food comes from plants and meat. They are called *omnivores*. These creatures can be secondary or tertiary consumers.

The top **predators** who are at the top of the food chain are lions, tigers, crocodiles, sharks and eagles. They haven't got any natural enemies. Can you think of one more top predator?

3 **Read** the text again. Match each living thing to a word in **blue**. Then order the photos to show a food chain.

a

Krill

b

Seal

c

Algae

d

Polar bear

e

Squid

c				

4 **Talk:** What is the **habitat** of the living things in Activities 1 and 3? What other animal habitats do you know?

5 **Use of English:** Find all the sentences with relative clauses in the text. Which relative pronouns are used? Complete the explanation below with each relative pronoun.

We use ¹_____ to talk about people and things; we use ²_____ to talk about people and we use ³_____ to show that something belongs to something or someone.

6 Work in a small group. Research and present a food chain.

- Choose two examples. Draw a diagram and practise explaining the food chain to each other. Use the words from the text, and relative clauses to describe the animals. Remember to mention their habitat and what type of animals they are.
- Present your diagrams to your class.

Key words: natural world

ecosystem: the way living things affect each other and the environment

link: a connection to something

diet: the food and drink that a living thing needs

predator: an animal that hunts and kills other animals for food

---

Use of English – Relative clauses

Defining relative clauses tell us which person or thing is being talked about. Relative clauses begin with a **relative pronoun: that, which, where, when, who, whose, whom.**

These creatures are small carnivores **whose** main diet is meat.

〉 3.3 The strange world of carnivorous plants

We are going to...

- explain key facts about carnivorous plants using wh- questions.

Venus flytrap

1   Talk: Look at the photos. What are carnivorous plants? How are these plants different to other plants?

 2   Listen to Part 1. Minh is explaining key facts about carnivorous plants. Check your answers for Activity 1.

> **Use of English – Wh- questions review**
>
> Question word + **do** + subject + **verb**
>
> What   do   you   **know** about carnivorous plants?

3   Use of English: Read the Use of English box and sort the words to make Minh's questions.

a   carnivorous plants / do / grow / Where / ?
b   these plants / Why / eat / other living things / do / ?
c   they / What / do / eat / animals / ?
d   does / How / its prey / catch / a carnivorous plant / ?

Sundew

 4   Pronunciation: Intonation in question forms. Listen and check your answers for Activity 3. Listen again and repeat.

> **Listening tip**
>
> **Prediction**
>
> Talk about what you already know about a topic. Try to predict what you will hear. Then listen for your ideas.

Pitcher

5   Talk: Read the Listening tip box. In pairs, make predictions about the answers to Minh's questions.

 6   Listen to Part 2 and check your predictions for questions a–c in Activity 3.

Butterwort

7 Listen to Part 3 about the Sundew plant. Check your predictions for question d in Activity 3. Then match the sentences below to the pictures.

1  2  3

a Then, the leaf curls around the insect and crushes it.

b When an insect crawls onto the leaves, it is trapped by the thick sticky liquid.

c The Sundew plant has long thin leaves covered in tiny hairs.

8 Vocabulary: Work in pairs. Describe to each other how the Sundew plant catches its prey. Use the words below to help you.

> leaves   hair   sticky   liquid   trap
> crush   juices   dissolve   digest

9 Talk: Read the Speaking tip box. How could Minh use these ideas for visuals in her presentation? Which idea do you like best? How would you use it?

10 Present it! **Explain the habits of a carnivorous plant.**

- Choose another carnivorous plant from Activity 1.
- Research key facts using Minh's questions.
- Use the questions to organise and write your presentation. Use the sentences and words in Activities 6 and 7 to help you.
- Create visuals to show how your plant traps its prey.
- Use the visuals to present your findings to your class.

Speaking tip

Use visuals

Visuals give everyone something to focus on in a presentation. They help the presenter to explain and the audience to understand the key facts.

You can use **diagrams, photos, a 3D model, real objects** or **videos.**

〉 3.4 Animal types

We are going to...

- **create an infographic text about a type of animal.**

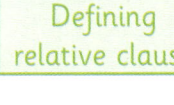

WHAT IS AN AMPHIBIAN?

Present simple

Amphibians are animals that can live in water and on land. They need a moist environment to survive. Their habitats are near water or in wet places.

Defining relative clause

Key words

Characteristics

Amphibians are **vertebrates**, which means they have a spine or back bone.

They have a smooth, thin skin, that feels moist and sticky.

Most amphibians have lungs and gills. Most can breathe and absorb water through their skin too.

Did you know...

... that the most toxic amphibians are very brightly coloured? Their colours warn other animals to stay away from them!

Types of amphibians

There are over 8,000 species of amphibians, including frogs, toads, salamanders and newts.

short sentences

Amphibians lay their eggs in water.
Their eggs are covered in a gel, not a shell.

The young developing amphibians must protect and feed themselves in the water.

When they develop legs and lungs, they move onto the land to live and return to the water to breed and find food.

1 **Listen** to the animal sounds. Can you identify the animals?
Classify the animals into types. Which type is missing?

Birds   Reptiles   Fish   Mammals   Insects   Amphibians

2 **Vocabulary:** Match the words below with the types of animals in
Activity 1. Which features can you see in the photos?

> breathe   fur   gills   lungs   scales   skin   fins   shell   feathers   egg

a   b   c

3 **Talk:** What type of animals can you see in the photos?
What are the similarities and differences between them?

The chameleon has scales but the whale has smooth skin.

4 **Read** the infographic text about amphibians.
Which of your points from Activity 3 are mentioned?

5 Find the key words underlined in the text and read the information.
Which information is new for you? Which is the most interesting?

6 Create an infographic text about a type of animal. Work in pairs.

Step 1: Choose an animal	Which animals are you interested in? Choose a specific animal or a group of animals.
Step 2: Research	Find out information about your animal using the internet or library. Use the key words in the text to guide your research. What are your animal's **characteristics**? What is its **habitat**? Make notes.
Step 3: Create the text	Use your notes to create sentences. Make the sentences concise and only include the most important information.
Step 4: Read and check	Proofread and edit your text; check and correct any errors.
Step 5: Create an infographic text	Find images to show the key points. Add your text to create your infographic.

> 3.5 Song for a Whale

We are going to...

- read a story about a connection between a girl and a whale.

1 **Talk:** What do you know about whales?
How do you think they communicate?

 2 **Read and listen** to the whole extract once.
How does this young girl find out about the whale's story?
What problem does the whale have?

Song for a Whale by Lynne Kelly

The narrator of the story is a young girl called Iris, who is deaf. In this extract, Iris is in class with her interpreter, Mr. Charles, who uses sign language to help her understand her teacher, Ms. Amarillo.

The video started out with a whale swimming in the ocean. Because of the captions, I could read the words on the screen instead of from Mr. Charles's hands. The dark gray-blue body of the whale filled up the screen, his tail waving up and down.

The narrator in the video talked about a whale called Blue 55, who swam around by himself and not in a **pod**, like other whales. As far as anyone knew, it had always been that way; he didn't have any friends or a family to swim with or talk to. He was a type of baleen whale – the type that ate **plankton** and small fish, not the kind with teeth that ate squid and seals. But he was a **hybrid**. His mother was a blue whale, and his father a fin whale.

3 **Read the extract again and decide if the sentences are true or false.**

a Iris was watching a video in class about a whale. true / false
b Mr Charles used sign language to help Iris understand the video. true / false
c The whale swam around in a group with other whales. true / false
d The whale's mother and father were different species. true / false

"The problem," said the narrator, "is Blue 55's unique voice. Most whales call out at **frequencies** of thirty-five hertz and lower, while this lonely whale's sounds are at around fifty-five **hertz**."

Only around 20 hertz off, but it made a big difference. He was speaking a language that only he knew.

"Furthermore, his song is in a unique pattern; even if the other whales can hear him, they don't understand what he is saying. Blue 55 probably can't communicate with his own parents."

My stomach tightened into a ball. I wanted another whale on the screen to swim up to Blue 55, or at least look at him.

"The strange calls of Blue 55 were first detected by **naval sonar** in the late 1980s. **Marine biologists** figured out what was making the sounds and why the whale was all alone in the **ocean**."

I didn't notice until the words on the screen blurred that my eyes were watery. Mr. Charles handed me a tissue from his pocket. Maybe I'd sniffled or something.

"Allergies," I signed, without looking away from the video.

Glossary

frequency: the number of times a sound is produced in one second

hertz: a unit of measurement of sound

naval sonar: equipment to find out where something is underwater

e The whale had a song that sounded very different to the other whales. true / false

f The other whales could still understand him. true / false

g Blue 55's own mother and father probably couldn't understand him. true / false

The narrator went on to say that researchers from a marine **sanctuary** had tried to put a **tracker** on Blue 55, so they could follow his migration pattern, which was also weird and unlike other whales'. They got a sample of his skin to test. That was how they figured out his parents had been different **species**. But, before they could attach the tracker to him, Blue 55 dove down and swam away. He wouldn't need to resurface for a breath for another twenty minutes. Without a tracker on him, the only way anyone ever knew where he was swimming was from underwater **microphones** that picked up his song.

I didn't remember standing up, but when the video ended and Ms. Alamilla started talking, I had to look down to see Mr. Charles. Everyone's eyes were on me as I slid back down into my chair. My textbook was on the floor – I must have knocked it off my desk when I stood up. I left it at my feet.

"Can you imagine that?" Ms. Alamilla asked. "Swimming around for all those years, unable to communicate with anyone?"

Yes.

She said something else about frequencies, but I wasn't paying attention anymore. I looked through Mr. Charles, as if I could still see that whale on the screen.

Blue 55 didn't have a pod of friends or a family who spoke his language. But he still sang. He was calling and calling, but no one heard him.

Glossary

tracker: a small device to record information about activity

microphone: equipment to record sound

h	People were trying to study Blue 55's characteristics and habits.	true / false
i	Iris paid attention to the teacher after the video had finished.	true / false
j	In the end, Blue 55 stopped trying to communicate with the other whales.	true / false

4 Work in pairs and correct all the false sentences.

5 **Vocabulary:** Match the marine wildlife words in blue to a definition.

    a   Very small plants and animals that bigger sea animals eat.
    b   A scientist who studies sea life.
    c   When animals travel to a different place.
    d   A group of whales.
    e   A very large area of sea.
    f   A safe place for animals.
    g   A group of animals that are very similar.
    h   A mixture of two very different things.

> **Language focus –
> Collective nouns**
>
> A **collective noun**
> is a group of
> specific things, for
> example, animals.
>
> A **pod** of whales.

6 Can you match the collective nouns to the correct animals?

1	A herd of	a	birds
2	A litter of	b	lions
3	A pack of	c	puppies
4	A flock of	d	wolves
5	A pride of	e	elephants

> **Reading tip**
>
> **Look at writing
> style**
>
> Understand the
> message in a
> story by looking
> at the author's
> writing style.

7 **Talk:** Use the words in Activity 5 to answer the questions.

    a   What was special about Blue 55's parents?
    b   What did the marine biologists want to study about Blue 55?
    c   Find three things that made Blue 55 different from
       other whales. Why couldn't he communicate?

8 **Read** the Reading tip box. Why do you think the author refers to Blue 55 as
'he' instead of 'it'? How does she want the reader to feel about Blue 55?

9 How did Iris feel when she was watching the video? Which words give you
clues about her emotions? Why do you think she felt like this?

10 **Values:** Feeling empathy.
Discuss the questions in pairs or in a small group.

    a   How did the story make you feel? Why?
    b   Iris had empathy with the whale. What do you think 'empathy' means?
       Choose the best definition.
       1   When you can understand someone's feelings because you can
          imagine their situation.
       2   When you love animals and nature.
       3   When you have the same problem as someone else.

    c   Think about situations at school and in class. How can it help to have
       empathy at these times? Think of three examples and tell your class.

⟩ 3.6 Project challenge

Project A: A presentation about how an animal survives

1   Work in small groups. Choose an animal for your presentation and brainstorm things you know already. Write four questions to find out about how it survives. Think about:

> **mammals   reptiles   amphibians   birds   insects   fish**

2   Research your animal using the internet or library. Use your questions to plan your research. Each group member should take a question to research. Here are some ideas for your questions:

> **habitat   hunting and prey   place in the food chain**
> **caring for young   climate**

3   Plan your presentation together. Use your questions to organise and write your presentation.

4   Create visuals to go with your presentation. Which visuals will engage your audience and make them want to listen and find out more? Think about:

> **videos   3D models   real objects   photos   diagrams/illustrations**

5   Check and practise your presentation together, using the visuals. Each group member should present a part.

6   Deliver your presentation as a group to your class, with each group member delivering a part.

Project B: Create a quiz about an animal

1   Work in pairs and choose an animal. Research information about your animal on the internet or in books or magazines. Find out about:

animal type   **features**   **habitat**   **how they survive**   **what they eat**

2   Write a quiz for another pair to answer.
   - Include at least one question about each of the topics in Activity 1.
   - You can include images too, e.g. photos, illustrations and diagrams.
   - Make sure you have noted down the answers!

3   Check your quiz questions. Check spelling and grammar and correct any errors.

4   Now write your quiz questions and add visual images. You can type or write the questions by hand (make sure your handwriting is clear and easy to read).

5   Swap your quiz with another pair and answer each other's questions. When you have all finished, get together to check your answers.

6   At the end, get together as a class and share two new pieces of information you have learned from each other's quizzes. Make a classroom display of the quizzes.

What materials did you use for your project? How did the materials improve your work?

> 3.7 What do you know now?

What do living things do to survive?

1 Write down three things that penguin families do to survive the extreme cold.

4 Why do carnivorous plants eat other living things? Describe one way that they trap their prey.

2 Choose an example of a food chain. How would you explain it to a younger child?

5 Describe three characteristics of an amphibian. Which characteristics do they share with other animal types?

3 What are herbivores, carnivores and omnivores? Explain to your partner.

6 In the story in Lesson 3.5, why does Iris have so much empathy with the whale in the video?

Look what I can do!

Write or show examples in your notebook.

I can talk about how penguin families survive in Antarctica.

I can use relative clauses to explain how a food chain works.

I can explain key facts about a carnivorous plant using wh- questions.

I can write an infographic text about a type of animal.

I can understand a story with an animal theme.

Check your progress 1

1 Read the clues and guess the words.

a This adjective means worried or anxious.

b This word describes the area around the street where you live.

c This noun means that you are pleased because you have done something good.

d You wear these to protect your eyes when you are swimming.

e This part of your body connects your foot to your leg.

f In football, this player stands by the net to stop the other team from scoring goals.

g A baby bird.

h Fish use these to 'breathe'.

i This word means a group of birds or sheep.

**2 Word race. Now add one similar word to match each sentence in Activity 1.
You have three minutes!**

a nervous, excited

3 Work in a small group. Take turns to throw a dice. Make a sentence about the picture next to the number on the dice. Score 2 points if 1) your sentence makes sense; 2) it is grammatically correct. The first person to get 10 points is the winner!

a

b

c

d

e

f

4 Work in pairs. Play a game to correct the sentences!

Student 1 is O and Student 2 is X. Roll a dice: highest number starts.

Choose a sentence, 1–9. If you can correct the sentence,
put your O or X in the box. The first person to get three in a line wins!

1 Has you finished yet?	2 Is Ethiopia the hottest country at our planet?	3 Dad asked me help him.
4 The rollercoaster was amazement!	5 If you eat fruit, your body get healthy vitamins.	6 You mustn't warm up before running.
7 In the Antarctic winter, the sun don't rise for two months.	8 Herbivores are animals what only eat plants.	9 What a carnivore eat?

5 Play the 10 questions game! Work in small groups and follow the instructions.

- Each person takes turns to think of a word from the topics below.
- The rest of the group asks **yes** / **no** questions to find out what the word is.
- Remember you can only ask a maximum of 10 questions.

Types of sport
Sports equipment
Parts of the body
Types of animals
Animal features

Does this animal eat plants?

Does it eat other animals?

Yes, it does.

No, it doesn't.

6 In pairs, interview each other. Find out three interesting things about your classmate that you didn't know before. Then tell your group.

Have you ever been on a rollercoaster?

Where was it?

7 Compare the stories in Units 1, 2 and 3. Which one did you like the best? Why?

I liked… because…

4 Inventions

We are going to...

- **talk** about our favourite gadgets and equipment

- **discover** more about robot technology

- **give** facts about robots using the past simple

- **present** an idea for a new invention using future tenses

- **write** about an important invention

- **read** a story about a young inventor.

Getting started

How have important inventions changed our lives?

a What kind of invention is the boy using in the photo?
b What do you think are the possibilities for this invention?
c How do you think inventors create something like this? Where do they get their ideas from?

 Watch this!

〉 4.1 Gadgets and us

We are going to...

- talk about our favourite gadgets and equipment.

1 What is your favourite gadget or piece of equipment? When do you use it? Why is it important to you?

2 **Vocabulary:** Test yourself with this quiz! Match the quiz questions to the pictures.

a

1 What can go as fast as 19 kilometres per hour?

2 What was called the Clasp Locker and the Separable Fastener before it got the name we now use?

3 People started using these in the 1860s – what are they?

4 What was first used in China over 1,000 years ago?

5 This was much bigger in 1973. It was 22 centimetres long and weighed 1.13 kilograms!

f

6 In 2019, Apple sold nearly 50 million of these. What is it?

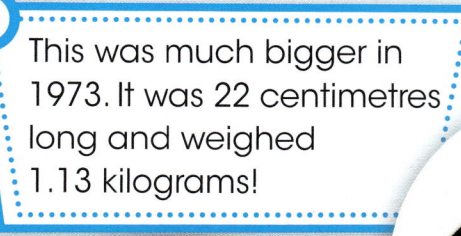

b

d

c

3 **Listen** to the children talking about favourite gadgets and equipment. Answer the questions.

   a Which gadgets or equipment from the quiz does each child describe?

   b Name two advantages and one disadvantage of each gadget.

> ### Listening tip
>
> **Listening for specific information**
>
> When you listen for the first time, listen only for the answers to the questions. Then listen again to understand more information.

 4 **Listen again and complete these sentences in your notebook. Who says what sentences, Lucia (L) or Ben (B)?**

   a It's _____ _____ _____ my tablet – I can't live without it!

   b I can _____ _____ _____ go online and message my friends.

   c The _____ _____ thing for me is my mountain bike.

   d I think it's _____ _____ _____ a bike.

   e It _____ _____ the type of bike.

5 **Write: What's the most important gadget or piece of equipment for you? Complete the sentences.**

   a It's got to be my _____ because I can use it _____.

   b I think it's _____ than a _____ because _____.

6 **Talk: Which 20th- and 21st-century inventions do you think are the most important? Have a pyramid discussion!**

   a In pairs, choose three important gadgets. What do you use them for? Why are they important? Make notes.

   b Make a group of four with another pair. Compare notes and decide together on the three most important items from your lists. Think of reasons why they are more important than the other items. Use the phrases in Activity 4 to help you.

> The most important gadget for me is... because...
> That's true but...

   c Present your ideas to the class. As a class, decide together on the three most important gadgets.

〉 4.2 Radical robotics

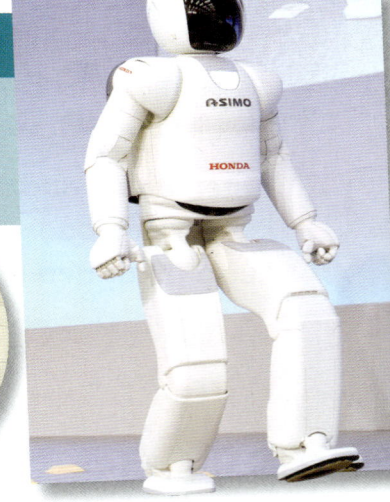

We are going to...

- discover more about robot technology
- give facts about robots using the past simple.

1 **Talk:** Look at the pictures of Asimo – a famous robot. Do you know anything about it? What do you think it can do?

 2 **Read and listen** to the article about Asimo and check your ideas from Activity 1.

Imagine a robot that can play football, dance, hop, jump and pour you a drink! Meet Asimo, the most advanced **humanoid** robot in the world. Asimo can walk on two legs and move by itself using **sensors** inside its body. It can understand voice commands and human gestures; it recognises moving objects and it can work out the distance and direction of those objects. It is just over one metre tall and has a rechargeable **battery**.

Scientists at Honda, the Japanese company, started developing Asimo in the 1980s and presented it to the world in 2000. The company created Asimo to help people in need with tasks around the house. Since then, scientists and designers have **upgraded** Asimo's technology, so it has more and more skills and abilities.

Asimo has become a worldwide celebrity and it has demonstrated its skills at science fairs and on TV shows all over the world! In 2005, Mickey Mouse welcomed Asimo at Disneyland. In 2011, it appeared on a TV quiz show in the UK, surprising everyone by dancing and pouring the presenter a drink; in 2014, it played football with the former US president, Barack Obama. It has even received royal welcomes in Dubai and the UK.

In 2018, Honda stopped producing the robot in its current form, but the company is continuing to use Asimo's technology to help people who need it most. Watch this space!

Reading tip

Use your own knowledge

Talk about the reading topic first. Then look for your ideas in the text.

Key words: design technology

humanoid: like a human

sensor: a device that detects objects nearby

battery: a device that produces electricity

upgrade: to change something to make it better

3 Work in pairs. What actions can Asimo do?
Take it in turns to mime the actions. You have one minute each.
How many actions can your partner guess?

4 **Read** the text again. Decide if these sentences are true or false.
Correct the false sentences.

    a   Most people knew about Asimo in the 1980s.
    b   Scientists created Asimo to do jobs for people with illnesses or disabilities.
    c   Asimo's technology was the same in 2014 as it was in 2000.
    d   In 2005, Asimo visited a famous theme park.
    e   Honda are still making Asimo robots.

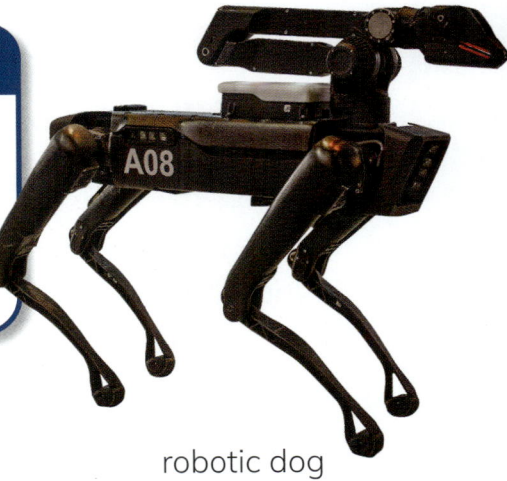
robotic dog

> **Use of English – Past simple review**
>
> We can use the **past simple** to talk about finished actions in the **past**. We often specify **when** something happened.
>
> Scientists **started** developing Asimo **in the 1980s**.
>
> **In 2014** it **played** football with the former US president...

5 **Use of English:** How many past simple verbs can you find in the text? When did each action happen? Find the time references.

virtual assistant

6 **Talk:** What other jobs do you think robots can perform? Look at the photos for ideas. Which jobs might be better for robots to do than humans?

snakebot

7 Work in small groups. Find out more about one of the robots in the photos.

    •   Who invented it? Why? What does it do?
    •   Choose two interesting facts to read out to your class. Can they guess which robot you are talking about?

Mars rover

> 4.3 Bright ideas

We are going to...

- present an idea for a new invention using future tenses.

1 Talk: If you could invent something new, what would it be? Look at the topics and think of ideas for new inventions. Compare with your partner.

> Communication   Transport
> Food   Comfort   Entertainment

Speaking tip

Organise your presentation

Organise your presentation into sections so your audience can follow the order clearly.

 2 Listen to the teacher talking before Kim's presentation. Who is Kim presenting her idea to? Why?

 3 Listen to Kim's presentation about her idea for a new invention. Which picture describes her idea?

a   b   c

 4 Listen again and put the headings in the order of the presentation.

a   How people will use the invention.
b   A summary of the idea.
c   Description of the idea.
d   Introduction and picture.

 5 Listen and complete the audience's questions.

a   How do you _____ on the Uber Jet Boots?

b   Where will you _____ to give the boots power?

6 Talk: What do you think about Kim's idea? Write two more questions to ask her.

7 Use of English: Read the Use of English box and choose the correct answers in bold below.

a With pronouns (*I, you, he, she, it, we, they*), the form of *will / won't* stays the **same / changes**.

b We use the **verb / verb + to** form after *will* and *won't*.

> **Use of English – *will* for future predictions**
>
> This invention **will change** the way people travel...
>
> People **won't crash** into each other...
>
> Which idea **will** the judges **choose**?

8 Think about Kim's presentation. Use the verbs in the box to complete the sentences.

| be | need to | solve | save | ~~be able to~~ | have |

1 You will <u>be able to</u> travel as fast as you like.

2 Will the boots _____ people money? Yes, they will!

3 Uber Jet Boots will _____ the traffic problems in our city.

4 You won't _____ travel by car any more.

5 You won't _____ so many traffic accidents.

6 The jet will _____ so powerful that you can stand up straight.

9 Present it! Choose and present a new invention.

- Choose one of your ideas from Activity 1, or a new idea. Make notes.
- Organise your notes into sections and add sequencing phrases.

  Today I'm going to talk about...

- Draw a picture showing your idea to introduce your presentation.
- Practise your presentation with a partner.
- Perform your presentation in front of your class. Some of the audience are going to be judges. Be prepared to answer their questions at the end.
- At the end, vote on the best idea in the class.

〉 4.4 Changing the world

We are going to...

- write about an important invention.

1 **Talk:** What do you think are the most important inventions of all time? Work with a partner. How many can you think of in one minute?

2 **Read:** Hassan's essay. Which invention does he discuss? What two things couldn't people do without this invention?

A world without wheels

In my opinion, the most important invention of all time is the wheel. Without the wheel, people could not travel anywhere very easily or quickly. We depend on the wheel for all our transport, **such as** cars, trains and planes (**because** planes need wheels to take off). It is very difficult to travel long distances without wheels. You would have to walk, or ride on a horse or camel! So we couldn't visit other cities and countries easily. **This means that** we couldn't find out about other places and our world would be very small.

We need the wheel so people can work easily and efficiently. **This is because** we need wheels to travel, but also **because** we need wheels to carry things. Of course, people can carry things in other ways, **for example**, by themselves or using animals. But this isn't very fast or efficient, especially if the things are heavy. Wheels are also a very important part of machines in factories and on farms **because** they make the machines work. These kinds of wheels are called 'cogs'.

There are lots of very important inventions that have changed the world, but **I think that** the wheel is the most important **for these reasons**.

3 **Read the essay again and answer these questions.**

a Why is it important for people to travel? What reasons does Hassan give?

b Why are wheels important for work? Find two reasons.

4 Word study: Giving opinions and reasons.
Look at the phrases in blue in the text.
Which phrase do you use before giving:

a ... your opinion In my opinion,
b ... a reason for your opinion
c ... examples?

5 How persuasive is Hassan's essay? What do you think is his strongest reason? Do you agree with his opinion?

6 Talk: Describe one of these inventions to your partner, but don't say the name! Use phrases from Hassan's essay and Activity 4. Can your partner guess what it is?

> the internet   satellites   clocks   television
> a writing pen   smartphones   USB stick

People need this invention so they can...

Without this invention, it is very difficult to... This means that...

7 Write a persuasive essay about an important invention.

Step 1: Research and make notes	Which do you think is the most important invention of all time? Why is it so important? What is your opinion and the reasons why? Think of two or three reasons to support your opinion.
Step 2: Planning	Start your essay by stating your opinion. Then give your reasons and examples. Start with the strongest reason. Use Hassan's model essay to help you. In my opinion, the most important invention of all time is the wheel.
Step 3: Writing	Organise your points using the phrases for giving opinions, reasons and examples. Remember, the aim is to persuade your readers to agree with your opinion!
Step 4: Read and check	Work with a partner. Proofread each other's work and circle any errors. Correct the errors and ask your teacher to check.
Step 5: Display or publish your essays.	Read each other's essays. Which one is the most persuasive? Take a class vote!

Writing tip

Support your opinions

When you give an opinion in an essay, support your opinion with reasons. The aim is to persuade the reader to agree with you!

> 4.5 Start Small, Think Big

We are going to...

- read a story about a young inventor.

1 **Talk:** Have you ever had a crazy idea? What was it? Did you tell anyone? What was their reaction?

2 **Read** and listen to the first part of the story. What was Garth's crazy idea?

3 Now read and listen to all the parts and answer the questions.

Start Small, Think Big
by Jane Boylan

1 Garth stood outside his house, **grinning** from ear to ear. He was **thrilled** at the rainy, windy October afternoon. This was perfect weather for testing his fabulous new invention – his Bodybrella – for the very first time. He carefully placed the Bodybrella over his head, fastened the head strap securely under his chin, and started **walking along** the street. He was so excited about his new invention and could hardly wait to try it out.

The Bodybrella was no ordinary umbrella. Ordinary umbrellas only kept the head dry. Not the Bodybrella! Garth's design covered his head and half his body in a magnificent transparent dome. It even left his hands free because the head strap kept it in place. It was a work of genius! He **strode** down the street, happily noticing that his invention worked wonderfully against the rain and the wind. He even passed a man wrestling with an umbrella, a bag of shopping and a yapping dog on a lead. The man stared open-mouthed as Garth calmly **walked past** him. He just knew the man was full of admiration at this amazing new device that kept your whole body dry and left your hands free. Soon everyone would want to own one!

a How did Garth feel about his invention?
b What problems did the invention answer?
c What did Garth do to test his invention?

> **Glossary**
>
> **grinning:** smiling a lot
> **thrilled:** very pleased
> **strode (stride):** o walk with a strong purpose

2 Then his heart sank. Striding towards him on the other side of the road were the Barker Boys, three nasty neighbourhood brothers. Garth turned quickly to run back home, but it was too late.

The three boys were soon standing around him, sneering with cruel delight. Todd, the biggest one, grabbed his Bodybrella and roughly pulled it off him. 'What's THIS?' he spat. 'It's a Bodybrella,' Garth squeaked. 'It covers your whole body and…' But the boys weren't listening. Instead, they were doubled over, howling with laughter. 'It looks dumb! Do you think anyone would wear that stupid thing?' Todd **sneered**, 'You're just a freak, Garth, living in a freak's dream world…' He tossed the Bodybrella over his shoulder and the three boys **ran off** shrieking with laughter. The mocking **jibes** rang in Garth's ears long after they were out of sight.

d Were the Barker Boys friendly or hostile towards Garth?

e What did Todd Barker do to Garth's invention?

f What was the boys' reaction to Garth's invention?

g What did Todd think of Garth's invention?

Glossary

sneer: to look at someone in a cruel way
jibes: cruel comments

3 Trembling and **humiliated**, Garth picked up his battered invention from the ground.
He could feel hot tears prickling his eyes. Maybe the **repugnant** Todd Barker was right…
In reality, who would ever want to wear his invention? He was just fooling himself…

Suddenly he **looked up** and saw a smart lady in a suit peering at him with concern.

'I was just leaving my house when I saw you and those boys. Are you okay?'

h How did Garth feel after his encounter with the Barker Boys?

i Who did he see next?

Glossary

humiliated: feeling stupid
repugnant: horrible, disgusting

4 Then she saw the Bodybrella in Garth's hand. It was broken now, **limp** and **grubby**. It looked like a crumpled jellyfish.

'Er… what's that?'

'It's my Bodybrella. I made it myself…' sighed Garth **wearily**, **waiting for** the lady to start laughing like the Barker Boys. But she gently took the object out of his hands, held it up and inspected it with interest.

'What an interesting idea! Did you think of it yourself?'

'Yes!' said Garth, suddenly brightening. Then, to his delight, the lady started asking him lots of questions about the Bodybrella, and how he had put it together.

j   What was the lady's reaction to Garth's invention?
k   How did he feel then? Why?

5 Finally she exclaimed, 'What a fine creative mind you have, Garth! If you can invent something so clever now, whatever will you be able to do when you're a grown-up? Don't let stupid ignorant boys like that put you down! Keep inventing and one day you will create something really marvellous!'

'And you've given me a fabulous idea,' she continued. 'I own a gadget shop – Gadgets4U – I'd like to run a competition to find the best young gadget inventor in our town. We must encourage wonderful creative minds like yours, Garth! I will display the three best inventions in my shop, and, as prizes, the inventors will each get a big fat voucher to spend on gadgets. I would really like you to enter my competition, Garth – I'm sure you'll have every chance of winning a prize. Will you **think about** it?'

Garth gasped in amazement. Gadgets4U was one of his favourite places in the whole world. The thought of having one of his inventions displayed in that wonderful place was too exciting for words. He thanked the lady and ran home to invent something fantastic for her competition. He suddenly felt much better and could already feel lots of new ideas bubbling up, ready to spring to life!

l   What advice did the lady give Garth?
m   What kind of competition did she want to organise? Why?
n   How did Garth feel at the end?

4 Talk: Discuss these questions about the story.

a   What do you think about the Barker Boys' reaction towards Garth and his invention? How would you react to Garth's invention?

b   How was the lady's reaction different?

c   What important point did the lady make?

d   Why do you think Garth felt better at the end?

> **Language focus – Prepositional verbs**
>
> Prepositional verbs have two parts: **verb** + **preposition.** The <u>object</u> always comes <u>after</u> the preposition.
>
> Garth calmly walked past him.
>
> (Garth calmly walked him past.)

5 Word study: Look at the prepositional verbs in blue from the story. Can you work out the meaning from the context of the story? Then choose the correct verb to complete the sentences.

a   The robber grabbed the woman's handbag and _ran off_ quickly.

b   Where are you going? _____ _____ me! I want to come too.

c   I don't know what to do. Can I _____ _____ it?

d   When we _____ _____ at the sky, we saw thousands of stars.

e   I was surprised when he _____ _____ me without saying hello.

f   _____ _____ the street until you get to the café, then turn right.

> think about
>
> ~~ran off~~
>
> walk along
>
> wait for
>
> looked up
>
> walked past

6 Pronunciation: Listen and repeat the a sounds from the story. What difference do you notice when pronouncing the a sound?

a   l**a**dy   ok**ay**   **a**ble   displ**ay**   f**a**vourite   pl**a**ce

b   str**a**p   h**a**nds   g**a**dget   b**a**g   st**a**nding   h**a**ve

7 Values: Believe in yourself.

1   Look at the sentences and discuss which ones you agree with.

   a   You shouldn't think of crazy ideas because everyone will laugh at you.

   b   Crazy ideas are pointless because they are not real.

   c   Feel free to have crazy ideas because they might turn into something good in the future.

2   When is it important to believe in yourself? Talk about the situations below and give reasons. Think of other situations.

   • When you are doing an exam.

   • When you are trying something new.

   • When you are in a competition.

❯ 4.6 Project challenge

Project A: A presentation about the history of an invention

1   Work in a small group. Research the history of one of these inventions (or your own idea) using the internet or the library.

phone   computer   writing pen

car   bicycle

2   Plan your presentation! Make notes about:
   - who invented it
   - the first models
   - how the invention has changed over the years
   - what the invention is like now.

3   Organise your notes into sections, using the headings in Step 2 above.
   Add other headings if you want to.

4   Add sequencing phrases from Lesson 4.3 to guide your audience through your presentation.

   Today, we're going to talk about...   To sum up...

5   Practise your presentation first in your group. Decide who is going to talk about each section. Think about questions that your classmates might ask at the end.

6   Add visuals to support the points in your presentation, e.g. photos or a video.

7   Deliver your presentation to your class. Answer your classmates' questions at the end. If you are listening to a presentation, write a question to ask at the end.

8   At the end, discuss how you think these questions will change in the future.

   In five years' time, I think phones will...

Project B: Create a quiz about inventions

1   Work in pairs. Research information about inventions in these categories.

medicine   transport   comfort or convenience   safety   communication

2   Write two or three questions or clues for each category.
Use the questions in Lesson 4.1 to help you.
For some of the questions, you can use pictures or photos, if you want to.

Your questions can be different styles, e.g.:

- Matching a question to a picture.
- A question with two or three possible answers (multiple choice).
- A true/false question.

3   Write a rough draft of your quiz.
Check grammar, vocabulary and spelling.

4   When you've checked your draft, write up your questions and clues on a large piece of paper. Make sure your handwriting is clear and decorate your quiz with photos and pictures.

5   Hand your quiz to another group to complete. Make sure you have an answer list, so you can check their work at the end.

What do you like about your project?
Is there anything you would improve next time? Why?

⟩ 4.7 What do you know now?

How have important inventions changed our lives?

1 Name five gadgets or pieces of equipment from Lesson 4.1.
Tell your partner which ones you use and why.

I use a... to.... I think it's more... than a...

2 Name three important events in the life of the Asimo robot in Lesson 4.2. Use the past simple.

3 Make four predictions about your town or city using **will/won't**.

4 Write four reasons why the wheel is so important in our lives.

5 Tell your partner about another invention that has changed the world. Think of four reasons why.

6 What did Garth invent in the story in Lesson 4.5. What was the reaction of the Barker Boys? What about the lady who owned the shop?

Look what I can do!

Write or show examples in your notebook.

	😑	😊
I can talk about and compare useful gadgets and pieces of equipment.	○	○
I can give facts about the Asimo robot using the past simple.	○	○
I can deliver a presentation about a new idea for an invention.	○	○
I can make future predictions using *will* and *won't*.	○	○
I can write a persuasive essay, giving my opinion and reasons.	○	○
I can read and understand a story about a young inventor.	○	○

5 ▶ Money

We are going to...

- **talk** about different ways to spend money

- **practise** being entrepreneurs

- **compare** ideas for spending a sum of money

- **discuss** whether children should get pocket money

- **read** about a boy who wants a special present.

Getting started

How can we use money in a good way?

 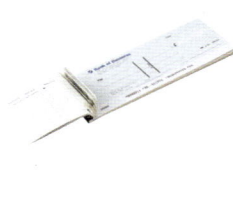 

a   Look at the photos. What different ways are there to pay for things?

b   Which are used most often? Which ones have you and your family used?

c   Do you have any money of your own? What do you do with it?

 Watch this!

5.1 Spending a sum of money

We are going to...

- talk about different ways to spend money.

Something to wear

1   **Talk:** Imagine you have some money to spend! How would you spend it? Are any of your ideas in the photos? Talk to your partner.

2   Try the Money Matters quiz! Circle the answer that you like best (don't show anyone your answers).

Money Matters Quiz

1   Do you think it is better to spend money on...
   a   having fun and exciting experiences?
   b   going shopping and buying things you like?

2   If you had some money to spend, would you buy...
   a   expensive trainers?
   b   cheap trainers and save the rest of the money?

3   You're going to give some money to a charity. It is a charity that helps...
   a   other children.
   b   animals and wildlife.

4   If you buy a new gadget or device (e.g. a tablet), should you buy...
   a   the most expensive one you can afford?
   b   a cheaper version so you have some money left?

5   If you have pocket money, you...
   a   save some of it for something special.
   b   spend it as soon as you have it!

Helping a charity

A day out

3   Work in pairs. Do the quiz again, but this time answer for your partner (don't show them the answers yet). Then compare answers. How well do you know your partner? Score one point for each correct guess!

Gadgets

4 **Listen** to some friends discussing one of the quiz questions. Which question are they talking about? Which opinion is the most similar to yours?

5 **Listen** again. Write down two reasons **for** buying expensive trainers and two reasons **against**. Can you think of any more reasons?

6 **Vocabulary:** Match the money words from the discussion to a definition.

1 a waste of money   a an organisation that provides money and help
2 afford   b spending money on something that isn't useful
3 last (v)   c to keep money to use in the future
4 a charity   d a type of product made by a particular company
5 save money   e to continue to be in good condition
6 a brand   f to have enough money to buy something

7 **Use of English:** Read the Use of English box and complete the sentences with comparative adverbs. Tick (✔) the sentences that you think are true.

more easily   more carefully
~~more quickly~~   longer
more often

> **Use of English – Comparative adverbs**
>
> We can use comparative adverbs with **verbs** to show change or compare how something is done.
>
> The expensive brands **are designed better**…
>
> … he **grows out** of them **less quickly** than me.

a I spend money _more quickly_ than I can save it.
b If something is made well, it usually lasts _____.
c I can save my pocket money _____ if I don't go shopping!
d It is better to spend your money on something you use _____.
e If you buy something yourself, you look after it _____.

8 **Talk:** Choose another quiz question from Activity 2 and discuss it in a group. Then share your opinions with your class. Use the vocabulary from Activity 6.

If you buy a new tablet, you should buy…   It's better to spend money on…
It's a waste of money to…   I'd buy a…

> 5.2 Clever calculations

We are going to...

- practise being entrepreneurs.

1 **Talk:** Have you ever done activities to raise money? What did you do? How was the money spent?

2 **Read:** Ava and Alex sold 95 chocolate brownies at the community fair and made a profit! Read the poster they made for their maths class.

    a   How many brownies did they make in total?
    b   Can you calculate their total **costs**?

> **Key words: calculations**
>
> **cost:** the amount of money
> **% (percent):** an amount of something out of 100 needed for something
> **kg (a kilogram):** 1,000 g

Brownies2go

There are several ways you can make chocolate treats, but we think this Brownie recipe is the best! Plenty of people agreed – we sold 95% of our brownies (with five left for us). Here's how we did it:

Ingredients for 100 chocolate brownies

	Cost	Sold (95%)	
1100g (1.1 kg) butter	$5.00	95 brownies $1.00 each	
1500g sugar	$1.00	TOTAL:	$95.00
16 eggs	$2.50		
300g cocoa powder	$1.00		
400g self-raising flour	$0.50		
400g chocolate chips	$3.00		
TOTAL: $13.00		PROFIT:	$95.00
+ paper bags (pack of 100 biodegradable)	$2.00	Minus total costs	$_____
TOTAL COSTS: $_____		TOTAL PROFIT:	$80.00

All profits from the community fair will go to two charities, either Polar Bear Rescue (50%) or Global Welfare (50%). Both of these charities do amazing work to help our planet.

Ava and Alex

3 **Read** the poster again. 50% of all money raised will go towards the charity Polar Bear Rescue. **Choose the correct answer.**

    1   What is 50% of Ava and Alex's **total profits**?   a $50.00 b $40.00

    2   How do you write 50% as a fraction?   a 1/2   b 1/5

4 Ava and Alex want to make 200 brownies for the next school fair.

    a   What are the new measurements for each ingredient? Calculate in grams and kilograms.

    b   What are the new costs of all the ingredients? What is the total?

    c   The children will need 200 paper bags. How much will the bags cost now?

    d   They manage to sell all 200 brownies (for $1.00 each)! How much profit do they make?

> ### Use of English – Quantifiers
>
> We use **several** and **plenty of** to describe amounts of things (we don't know exactly how much). **Either… or** and **both of** always refer to 'two'.

5 **Read** the **Use of English** box and find examples of the quantifiers in the poster. **Then choose the correct words to complete the explanation below:**

plenty of means [1]**lots of / a smaller amount** (e.g. 3 or 4);

several means [2]**lots of / a smaller amount** (e.g. 3 or 4).

6 **Present it!** Work in a small group. Create an activity to raise money for charity at a community event. Follow the instructions below.

- Decide which charity you want to raise money for.
- Brainstorm ideas for a product to sell, e.g. something to eat, drink, wear, read, play with, etc. What quantity will you produce?
- Calculate the costs of making the product. Make a list of things you will need, quantities and prices. Find out which places will supply your things at the cheapest price.
- If you sell all of your product, how much profit will you make?
- Present your idea on a poster. Think of a name for your product. Present calculations showing costs and profit. Use Ava and Alex's poster to help you.

> 5.3 Spending plans

We are going to...

- compare ideas for spending a sum of money.

1 **Talk:** What ideas for raising money can you see in the photos? Which do you like best? Can you think of any other ideas?

 2 **Listen** to the class discussion and answer the questions.

   a   Which activity did they do?
   b   How much money did they raise?
   c   What suggestion does Nacho make? Why?

 3 **Listen** to the next part of the discussion.
   How does Nacho's classmate, Marina, respond to his idea?

4 **Listen** again. What other ideas do the classmates have?
   What reasons do they give to support their ideas?
   Which idea do you like best? Why?

5 How much is $825 US in the currency of your country?

6 Read the Speaking tip box. Match the phrases (a–d) from the discussion with a function (1–4).

1 Introducing your point
2 Encouraging other people to respond
3 Agreeing
4 Partly agreeing

a 'What does everyone else think?'
b 'We think we should spend the money on...'
c 'We think it's a good idea to buy sports equipment but not for the table tennis club.'
d 'We agree with that.'

7 Listen and complete the phrases for making suggestions. Which phrases are followed by verb + -*ing*?

a _____ hear your ideas.
b _____ spending it on our end-of-term celebration?
c _____ using a small amount of the money for...?
d _____ use the money for a school trip?

> **Speaking tip**
>
> **Negotiating**
>
> In a discussion, use phrases to introduce your points, make suggestions and respond to other people too.

8 What role does the teacher have in the discussion? Choose adjectives from the box to describe how the teacher and students communicate.

> formal   informal   polite   rude   aggressive   friendly

9 Talk: In small groups, discuss a 'money' question.

• Brainstorm ideas for spending $825 on something for your class or school.
• Choose your favourite idea and think of reasons to support it. Practise explaining your ideas to your class. Use the phrases for introducing your point and making suggestions.
• Now discuss your ideas with your class. Your teacher will guide the discussion. Remember to use the phrases in Activities 6 and 7 to express your ideas and respond to your classmates.

⟩ 5.4 The question of pocket money

We are going to...

- discuss whether children should get pocket money.

1 **Talk:** What is pocket money? Do you get pocket money from your family? How do you decide how much?

2 **Read** 11-year-old Ismail's essay discussing children and pocket money. What is his opinion?

1 **Should children get pocket money?**

Across the world, there are different ideas about giving pocket money to children. Should children do jobs in the house for their pocket money? Should they have any pocket money at all? **In my opinion**, children should have pocket money **because** it teaches us useful things about money.

2 **Firstly**, when you have pocket money you learn how to spend money in a good way. You have to decide what to buy and what not to buy, **because** you can't buy everything you want! **Secondly**, when you buy things yourself, you learn about how much things cost. It makes you compare prices and find ways to buy things more cheaply. **And** if you want to buy something big, you learn how to save up for it. You don't have to ask your parents for it (and they might say no!)

3 **However**, some parents say that children already have everything they need, **therefore** they don't need pocket money. **But**, if you don't buy anything yourself, you don't appreciate the cost of things. Last year, I saved and bought a video game myself. I didn't know how expensive they were until I bought one for myself!

4 **Finally**, I think pocket money is a very good idea **because** it teaches us to manage money ourselves. This is important as we get older and when we are adults too.

3 **Read** Ismail's essay again. Find three reasons he gives to support his opinion. Find one real-life example.

4 Match the descriptions to paragraphs (1–4).

    a Conclusion: summarises the main point.

    b Introduction to the main point of view: what is the essay about?

    c One point against the main opinion.

    d Points to support the main opinion.

5 **Talk: Do you agree with Ismail's opinion? Think of more reasons why children should or shouldn't have pocket money.**

6 **Use of English: Find more examples of reflexive pronouns in the essay.**

7 **What do connecting words do in the essay? Match the numbered words in colour in the essay with a function.**

    a introduces your opinion

    b shows the order of points

    c adds another point

    d gives a reason

    e shows contrasting points

8 **Write an opinion essay. Choose one of the titles below:**

    a Should children do jobs to earn pocket money?

    b Should you get a lot more pocket money if you are older?

Language focus – Reflexive pronouns

We often use **reflexive pronouns** to draw attention to the person or people we are talking about.

Last year I saved and bought a video game myself.

… it teaches us to manage money ourselves.

Writing tip

Connecting words

Use **connecting words** to organise your ideas logically and help readers follow the points in your essay.

Firstly, when you have pocket money you…

… I think pocket money is a very good idea **because** it teaches us to manage money ourselves.

Step 1: Make notes	What is your opinion? Write points to support your opinion and one or two contrasting points. Try to think of at least one real-life point to support your opinion.
Step 2: Organise your essay	• Use the headings in Activity 4 to organise the information. • Use connecting words.
Step 3: Read, compare and check	• Swap with a partner. Did you have similar ideas? • Check for spelling and grammar mistakes!

〉 5.5 Billionaire Boy

We are going to...

- read about a boy who wants a special present.

1   **Talk:** How rich is a billionaire? What do you think are the advantages and disadvantages of having a lot of money?

 2   **Read and listen** to the first part of the story. It is the Billionaire Boy, Joe Spud's birthday. What special present would he like? Then read again and answer the questions.

Part 1

Billionaire Boy by David Walliams

The house was so large it was **visible** from outer space. It took five minutes just to **motor up** the drive. Hundreds of newly-planted, hopeful trees lined the mile-long **gravel track**. The house had seven kitchens, twelve sitting rooms, forty-seven bedrooms and eighty-nine bathrooms.

Even the bathrooms had **en-suite** bathrooms. And some of those en-suite bathrooms had en-en-suite bathrooms.

Despite living there for a few years, Joe had probably only ever explored a quarter of the main house. In the endless grounds were tennis courts, a boating lake, a helipad and even a 100m ski-slope complete with mountains of **fake** snow. All the taps, door handles and even toilet seats were solid gold. The carpets were made from mink fur, he and his dad drank orange squash from priceless antique medieval **goblets**, and for a while they had a **butler** called Otis who was also an orang-utan. But he had to be **given the sack**.

a   Why is it possible to see Joe's house from space?

b   How much of his home is familiar to Joe? Why is this?

c   What expensive materials are the taps and carpets made of?

Glossary

visible: you can see it
gravel track: a driveway or path made of very small stones
en-suite: attached to a bedroom
goblet: a special glass for drinks
butler: a type of servant
given the sack: to lose your job

"Can I have a *proper* present as well, Dad?" said Joe, as he put the cheque in his trouser pocket. "I mean, I've got loads of money already."

"Tell me what you want, son, and I'll get one of my **assistants** to buy it," said Mr Spud. "Some solid gold sunglasses? I've got a pair. You can't see out of 'em but they are very expensive."

Joe yawned.

"Your own speedboat?" ventured Mr Spud.

Joe rolled his eyes. "I've got two of those. Remember?"

"Sorry, son. How about a quarter of a million pounds worth of **WHSmith** vouchers?"

"Boring! Boring! Boring!" Joe stamped his feet in **frustration**. Here was a boy with high-class problems.

Mr Spud looked **forlorn**. He wasn't sure there was anything left in the world that he could buy his only child. "Then what, son?"

Joe suddenly had a thought. He **pictured** himself going round the **racetrack** all on his own, racing against himself.
"Well, there is something I really want…" he said, tentatively.

"Name it, son," said Mr Spud.

"A friend."

d   Why doesn't Joe think the cheque is a suitable present?
e   Why isn't the speedboat a suitable present?
f   How does Joe feel about the shop vouchers as a present?
g   What do you think 'high-class problems' are?
h   What is the only present that Joe wants?

 3   **Before you read the next extract, think of ways Joe could make his wish happen. Then read the next part. Are his ideas the same as yours? Answer the questions.**

Glossary

assistant: someone who helps someone else to do a job
WHSmith: a chain of book and stationery shops in the UK
racetrack: a road where you drive a racing car

Part 2

"I want to go to a different school, Dad," said Joe.

"No problem. I can afford to send you to the **poshest** schools in the world. I heard about this place in Switzerland. You ski in the morning and then —"

"No," said Joe. "How about I go to the local **comp**?"

"*What*?" said Mr Spud.

"I might make a friend there," said Joe. He'd seen the kids **milling** around the school gates when he was being **chauffeured** to St Cuthbert's. They all looked like they were having such a great time – chatting, playing games, swapping cards. To Joe, it all looked so fabulously *normal*.

"I could build you a school in the back garden if you like?" offered Mr Spud.

"No. I want to go to a normal school. With normal kids. I want to make a *friend*, Dad. I don't have a single friend at St Cuthbert's."

"But you can't go to a normal school. You are a billionaire, boy. All the kids will either bully you or want to be friends with you just because you are rich."

"Well, I won't tell anyone who I am. I'll just be Joe. And maybe, just maybe, I'll make a friend, or even two…"

Mr Spud thought for a moment, and then relented. "If that's what you really want, Joe, then OK, you can go to a normal school."

a   What kind of school does Joe want to go to? What is his Dad's reaction?
b   What does Mr Spud offer to do?
c   Why does Joe want to go to this type of school?
d   What problems does Mr Spud think Joe will have at this school? Why?
e   What is Joe's solution?
f   What does Mr Spud say in the end?

Glossary

comp: a comprehensive school (free)

4 Vocabulary: Match the words in blue with their synonyms. Why do you think the author uses these words instead of the synonyms (1–9)?

1 false	4 real	7 anger
2 saw	5 standing	8 driven
3 sad	6 drive	9 high quality

5 Read the sentences with idioms about money. Which ones describe Mr Spud? What do you think the idioms mean?

a He has more money than sense.
b He has a job that pays peanuts.
c He has money to burn.

6 Talk: Work in a small group. Read the story again and discuss the questions together.

a Would you like to live in Joe's house? Why? Why not?
b Do you think Joe's wealth is a positive or negative thing?
   What do you think the author wants us to think?
   Find clues in the story.
c Do you agree with Mr Spud that it will be difficult for Joe
   to make friends at his new school? Why? Why not?

7 Pronunciation: 's' sounds: Listen and repeat the words from the story. Which words have a soft 's' sound (/s/) and which have a hard sound (/z/)? Then put the words into two groups: /s/ and /z/.

1 vi**s**ible	3 **s**even	5 handle**s**	7 **s**on	9 problem**s**
2 hou**s**e	4 mountain**s**	6 **s**olid	8 pound**s**	

8 Values: Spending money wisely

a Work with a partner. Can you remember five things from the story that the Spuds own? Are these important things to have? Which of these things do you think they **need**?
b Look at the items in the box. Do you think they are things that people **want** or **need**?

> **a tablet   a new games controller   famous brand trainers   a hoverboard**

c Now choose one of these items and find out how much it costs.
   How long would it take you to save your pocket money to buy it?
d Think of something that you or your family have saved for.
   What was it? How did you feel when you finally bought it?

Reading tip

Powerful words and idioms

In stories, authors use **powerful descriptive words** to help you imagine the scenes. Sometimes these words are not so common in everyday speaking.

Idioms are phrases where the words have a different meaning together than individually.

But he had to be **given the sack**. (lose his job).

〉 5.6 Project challenge

Project A: Design a banknote

1 Work in pairs. Look at some examples of real cash currency from your country. What are the notes and coins made of? What images can you see?

2 Look at the banknotes. What different amounts are there? Do you know who any of the people are? Why do you think their images are featured on the notes?

3 You are going to design a new banknote. Brainstorm ideas and answer the questions:
   • What is the amount of your banknote?
   • Who will you feature? Why?
   • What other images and features will you put on the note?

4 Design your banknote using a collage of images. You can use drawings, photos, online images, cut-outs from newspapers and magazines, and patterns – be creative!

5 Make a poster to display your design. Write short texts to explain each design feature. Explain in detail why you have chosen the main images.

6 Make a classroom display of the posters. Look at your classmates' designs and note down your favourite, with the reason why, to share with your class at the end.

Project B: Making money grow for a good cause

1   Work in a small group. Imagine someone has given you $50 (US) in your currency. (How much is this?) You are going to use the money to help others.
    Brainstorm ideas and answer the questions:
    • Who would you like to help? Why?
    • How can you grow the $50 into a bigger amount? Think of a product or service to invest the money in.

2   When you have an idea, work out how you will use the $50 to make the idea happen. Here are some ideas to help you:
    • Buy things to sell.
    • Buy things to make something to sell (like ingredients for cakes).
    • Use the money to help you provide a service.
    • Remember, you must use all the money! Anything left over will be taken away.

3   Work out the costs involved in making your idea happen. Then work out what profit you will make. Make a chart to show your calculations.

4   How will your profit help others? Show ways the money can be used.

5   Create a presentation to show your idea to your class.
    Deliver your presentation, with each group member taking a turn.
    • Explain your idea, who you are going to help and why.
    • Show your calculations for costs and profit.
    • How will the money be used?

6   As a class, compare all the ideas. Is there one that you could all do to raise money for a good cause?

Which skills did you develop in your project?

91

> 5.7 What do you know now?

How can we use money in a good way?

1 Tell your partner about…

- something you think is a waste of money
- a brand you like
- a charity you admire

4 Write down two reasons why Ismail thought children should get pocket money in Lesson 5.4.

2 Talk to five friends. What percentage of the group get pocket money? What percentage don't save any money?

5 Where does the Billionaire Boy, Joe Spud, want to go to make new friends? Why doesn't his dad think it is a good idea?

3 Look back to Lesson 5.3.
  a How much money did the class raise?
  b If they spend all the money on three small laptops, how much would each one cost?
  c If they spend 90% of the money on a school trip, how much is left?

6 Do you think Joe's dad, Mr Spud, spent his money wisely? Can you think of better ways he could spend his money?

Look what I can do!

Write or show examples in your notebook.

I can talk about different attitudes to spending money.

I can complete sentences with the correct comparative adverbs.

I can make calculations to work out costs and profit.

I can make sentences with different quantifiers.

I can discuss different ideas for spending a sum of money.

I can discuss questions about pocket money.

I can read and understand a story about having a lot of money.

6 ▶ People and work

We are going to...

- **talk** about why people do the jobs they do
- **design** a uniform for a job
- **discover** what it's like to be an astronaut
- **use** reported speech to describe someone's job
- **write** a job advertisement
- **read** and **enjoy** a poem about jobs and work.

Getting started

Why do people do their jobs?

a   What activities are the children doing?
b   What talents and skills do they need to do these activities?
c   What kind of jobs do you think they might have when they are older?

Watch this!

> 6.1 How do you get a job?

We are going to...

- talk about why people do the jobs they do.

1   **Talk:** What kind of jobs do people in your family have?
    Do they like their jobs? Why? Why not?
    What job did they want to do when they were young?

2   **Vocabulary:** Match the photos to the words in the box.
    Do you know anybody who has these jobs?

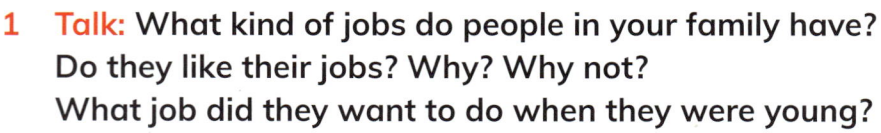

marine biologist   physiotherapist   engineer
computer programmer   science teacher   vet

41   3   **Listen** to these people describing how they got their jobs.
         Which jobs are they talking about?

     4   **Talk:** Which job do you think sounds the most
         interesting? Why? Which job relates to skills that you have?

5 **Vocabulary:** Compound nouns.
Can you find five compound nouns
in the word puzzle?

**Language focus –
Compound nouns**

A compound noun is
two words together.
website   science teacher

6 Can you complete the definition of a **compound noun**?
Use the Language focus box and your answers for Activity 5 to help you.

> The first word is usually a noun or an [1]_____ .
> It describes the second word, which is a noun.
> Compound nouns can be one word, e.g. [2]_____ ; or two words, e.g. [3]_____ .

7 Find out the meaning of these compound nouns.
How do you think these things can help you get a job?

> work experience   ·   voluntary work   university degree

41

8 **Listen:** Look at the comments about interests and
abilities. Can you match each one with a job from
Activity 2? Then listen again and complete the
comments with the correct adjective or preposition.

a   I've been _____ about animals ever since
I was a little girl.
b   I had to work really hard _____ maths and
science.
c   I became more interested _____ coding...
d   I was always really _____ on sport at school...
e   I was always fascinated _____ the ocean...

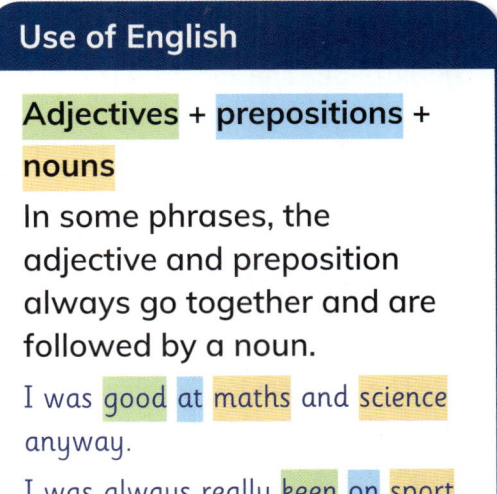

Use of English

Adjectives + prepositions +
nouns

In some phrases, the
adjective and preposition
always go together and are
followed by a noun.

I was good at maths and science
anyway.

I was always really keen on sport.

9 **Talk:** What kind of job would you like to do?
What interests and talents do you have now
that might lead to a job in the future?
Explain to your partner, using the phrases in Activity 8.

I'm really good at fixing things, so I'd like to be an engineer or a...

95

> 6.2 Designs that work!

We are going to...

- **design a uniform for a job.**

1 **Talk:** What do people wear for these jobs in your country?
What do their uniforms look like?
What other jobs do you know where people wear a uniform?

> firefighter   police officer   nurse   postman/postwoman   chef

2 **What things do designers think about when they design a uniform?**

The climate and weather in the country where they work...

 3 **Read and listen** to Seb's description of his design for a work
uniform. Which job in Activity 1 is the uniform for?
Which of your ideas from Activity 2 are mentioned?

My new uniform is like a tracksuit, dark blue with a green and
white **stripe** along the shoulders and down the **sleeves**. The
white stripe is **reflective**, to show up when there isn't much light
outside. The jacket has a **zip** and **inside pockets**, to keep money
and other small things. It also **features** the post office **logo** on
the front right at the top. The trousers are quite wide, with
waterproof material from the ankle to the knee, so, if the ground
is wet, the bottom of the trousers stays dry. The trousers have zips at the
bottom and **zipped pockets** on the side. There are comfortable **trainers** for the
feet, because you have to walk a lot in this job.

The uniform has a cap with a **light** on the front, so the postman or woman can
switch this on if they are working when it is dark. And there is a special **belt with
pockets** to carry things like phones or keys; this leaves the person's hands free to
deliver the post. The belt also holds an **alarm**, which makes a loud sound which can
protect the person from aggressive dogs or other dangers.

My uniform design will **suit** people who are all shapes and sizes – big or slim, tall
or short – because the design is loose-fitting and the **fabric** is stretchy.
I hope everyone who wears my design will feel comfortable and smart!

4 Vocabulary: Match the words in blue in the description with the letters, a–k, on the picture.

> **Key words: design**
>
> **reflective:** shows up in the dark
>
> **feature:** an important part of something
>
> **suit:** to be suitable for a purpose or situation
>
> **fabric:** cloth or material for making clothes

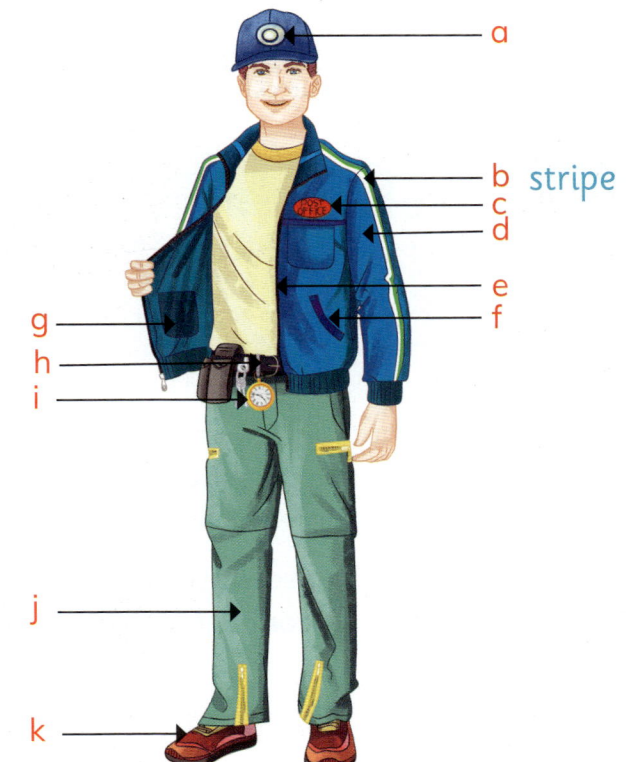

a

b stripe
c
d

e
f

g
h
i

j

k

5 Read the description again.
What features are there in Seb's design which help with these things?

- climate and weather
- safety
- carrying personal things
- comfort

6 Talk: What do you think of Seb's design? How does it compare with what postmen and postwomen wear in your country? Would you change anything to better suit your country?

7 Present it! In groups, think about a uniform in your country that you would like to change. Follow the instructions.

- Choose a uniform. It could be a work uniform, a sports kit or your school uniform.
- Draw a picture of your idea and label the features.
  Think about issues mentioned in Activity 5 in your design.
- Prepare a description to present your idea.
  Explain the reasons for the main features.
  As you can see, there is a... because...
- Present your idea to your class, with each group member taking a turn.
  At the end, vote on the most interesting and practical design idea!

❯ 6.3 Working in space

We are going to...

- discover what it's like to be an astronaut
- use reported speech to describe someone's job.

1 **Talk:** Look at the photo of an astronaut doing a spacewalk. What is happening in the photo? What challenges are there for the astronaut?

2 **Vocabulary:** What do these words mean? How do you think the words are connected with astronauts and their work?

> spacewalk   experiments   gravity   exploration   risky

Astronauts often do experiments in space...

43 3 **Listen** to the interview with Karina, an American astronaut. Check your ideas from Activities 1 and 2.

43 4 **Listen again.** Are the statements about Karina's interview true or false?

a	Karina says that she has always been interested in space exploration and science.	true / false
b	She says that astronauts can't do experiments in space because there isn't any gravity.	true / false
c	She explains that research in space today will help space travel in the future.	true / false
d	She tells us that she loves doing spacewalks inside the space station.	true / false
e	She says that astronauts get taller in space because their legs get longer.	true / false

---

Use of English – Reported speech

Direct speech	Reported speech
'I have done three spacewalks so far.'	**Karina says that** **she has done** three spacewalks so far.
	She doesn't say that she has done one spacewalk.

---

5 **Use of English:** Check your answers to Activity 4.
Correct the false sentences using reported speech.

Karina didn't say that... She said that...

 6 **Vocabulary:** Personal qualities. Listen to the next part of the interview.
Put the adjectives in the order that you hear them.

> confident   exciting   fit   enthusiastic   adventurous   hardworking

7 Match the adjectives in Activity 6 with their opposites.

a boring   b unfit   c unadventurous
d lazy   e shy   f unenthusiastic

8 How many of the opposite adjectives are made with a prefix? Play a game!
What other adjectives do you know with prefixes? You have one minute!

9 **Talk:** What have you learned from the interview with Karina?
Tell your partner something that you didn't know before.

10 **Write** other questions you would like to ask an astronaut about their work.
Imagine their answers. Work in pairs. Share your questions and answers
with your class.

11 **Interview** someone you know about their job. Then report back to your class.

- What do you do in your job?
- What is your favourite part of your job?
- What's the strangest thing you've learned in your job?
- What qualities and skills do you need to do your job?

12 Tell your class about your interview using reported speech.

My uncle said that he...   My mum told me that she...

❯ 6.4 Let's get a job!

We are going to...

- write a job advertisement.

1 **Talk:** How do people find jobs? With your partner, think of three different ways someone could find a job.

2 **Read:** Match the job titles in the box to the adverts.

zookeeper   acrobat   inventor

Could you invent the world's next best-selling gadget?

We are looking for a genius-level _____ to form a dynamic new team.

- Must be able to do experiments.
- Must be fascinated by science.
- For further details, please visit our website.
- Interviews will be held in the time machine.

present continuous

We are looking for an enthusiastic _____ to join our troupe.

No pronoun

- **Must be** very flexible, strong and athletic.
- Must be able to balance on one leg.
- Must be good with heights.
- Interviews will be held on the tightrope.

We are looking for a friendly _____ to lead our team of animal carers.

- 🐾 Experience needed – this job is more challenging than it looks!
- 🐾 Must be interested in ALL kinds of animals (not just the cute and cuddly).
- 🐾 Must be brave and comfortable with big teeth and claws.
- 🐾 Interviews will be held in the lion enclosure.

3 Read the adverts again. Which of these candidates are most suitable for the jobs in Activity 2? Which one is not suitable for any jobs?

a Priya is very keen on design and technology.

b Finn is really good at gymnastics.

c Zainab is fascinated by biology and natural science.

d Hugo is very interested in history and maths.

4 **Use of English:** Read the Use of English box. How would the sentences change with the pronouns, *I* and *he/she*?

5 Look at the advert. Find and correct the mistakes. What sentences can be shortened?

> **Use of English – Present continuous review**
>
> We use the present continuous to talk about something which we think is temporary and is happening now.
>
> **We are looking** for a friendly zookeeper...
> **We are recruiting** genius-level inventors...

> **Writing tip**
>
> **Use shortened sentences in adverts**
>
> ~~You~~ Must be able to do experiments. Experience needed...

Gardener

Are you good with a spade? We is looking for a talented gardener.

- You must be crazy about flowers and plants.
- You must be calm and not afraid of bugs and insects.
- Experience is needed.
- We are interview now. Call us on 6976 5454.

6 **Write** a job advert.

Step 1: Write notes	• Brainstorm unusual jobs. What skills are needed?
Step 2: Write an advert	• Write a short introduction to get the reader's attention. We are looking for... • Write sentences asking about skills and talents. Mention the interview place. Use shortened sentences and the present continuous. Draw a picture. Must be good at...
Step 3: Read and check	• Proofread your advert; check and correct any errors.
Step 4: Display your advert	• Put your job advert on the wall. Walk around and read other adverts. Then choose one job that you would like to do.

❯ 6.5 You can be anything

We are going to...

- read and enjoy a poem about jobs and work.

1 **Talk:** When you are older, what kind of job would you like to have? A creative or practical job? Or a job helping other people?

 2 **Read and listen** to the poem. Does the poem mention jobs that you talked about in Activity 1? Match the pictures to jobs in the poem.

You can be anything
by Teri Hopkins

… See you can be anything, but you must try,
So never give up, REACH for the sky.
You could be a doctor and look after the sick,
Or a builder building houses, brick after brick.
You could be a dentist and fix a cracked tooth,
Or look after horses, mending sore **hooves**.
You could be a singer singing songs to a crowd,
Have everyone screaming your name out aloud.

See you can be anything, but you must try,
So never give up, REACH for the sky.
You could be an actor and dress up all day,
Pretend to be different, whoever you may.
You could be a hairdresser and cut people's hair,

a

b

Cut all sorts of shapes, whatever you dare!
You could be a plasterer and smooth **wonky** walls,
On ceilings in bedrooms in kitchens and halls.
See you can be anything but you must try,
So never give up, REACH for the sky.
You could be a firefighter, and save someone's life,
Putting great big fires out, morning till night.
You could be a police officer patrolling the roads,
Keeping the world safe from the bad boys and girls,
You could be a scientist making potions and pills,
Finding new medicines that help mend the ill.

See it really doesn't matter whatever you choose,
As long as you're happy you will never lose,
But don't look at me to decide what you do,
The only one making that choice will be…
YOU!

Glossary

hooves: horses' 'feet'
wonky: bumpy, uneven

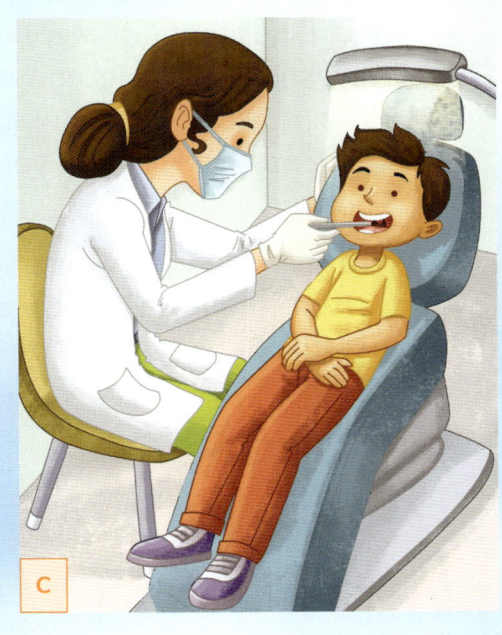

c

d

e

103

POLIC

 3 **Read and listen to the poem again.
Discuss these questions in groups.**

   a How many jobs does the writer mention?
Are any of the jobs similar?

   b What point is the writer making by writing
about jobs that are very different?

   c How should you feel about your job?
What advice does the writer give?

   d What other advice can you think of?
Share your ideas with your class.

4 **Word study: Find ten words for jobs in the poem and look at the
suffix (the ending). Then divide them into groups according to
their suffix. Can you add five more jobs? Look at other lessons
to help you.**

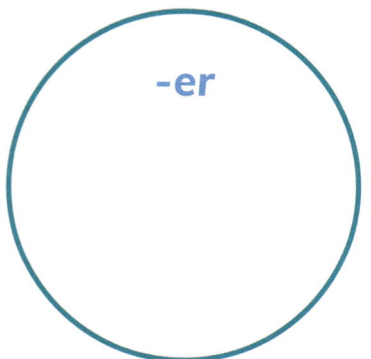

-er

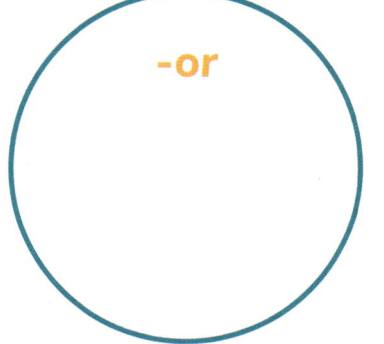

-or

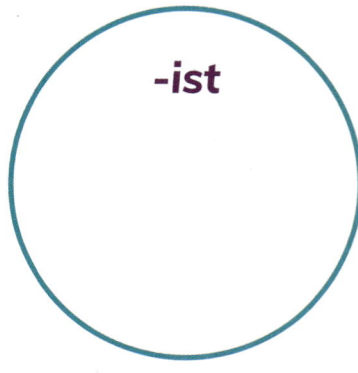

-ist

 5 **Pronunciation: Listen to the second verse of the poem again.
What rhyming vowel sounds do you hear at the end of each line?**

 6 **Say these words and match to the sounds
in Activity 5. Listen and check.**

> way   my   falls   share

Language focus – could (+ be)

You **could be** a doctor and look
after the sick.

You **could be** a dentist and fix a
cracked tooth.

7 **Use of English: Choose the correct definition
of could.**

   a You are *allowed* to be a doctor or dentist.

   b You will *definitely* be a doctor or dentist.

   c It is *possible* that you will be a doctor or dentist.

8 Write: Use the pictures to make two more sentences using the structure in the poem. Make the sentences rhyme! Then make two more sentences with your own ideas.

You could be a _____ who _____.

You could be a _____ who _____ and _____.

You could be a _____ who _____.

You could be a _____ who _____.

9 Values: Working hard and setting goals

a   Have you ever worked hard to achieve something?
    How did you feel? Tell your partner. Use these topics to help you.
    - A sport or after-school activity
    - A school project or exam
    - Music, art, video or theatre

b   Look at Amir's notes about something he wants to achieve. What do you think it is?

c   What actions is Amir going to take to achieve his goal?

- Practise every day – half an hour before school + Saturday mornings.

- Tell Dad and Jamil so they can help me.

- Go to United match on 28th Aug – watch strikers.

- Sign up for trial for under-12s for new school team.

Trials: 10th and 11th Sept.

d   What goals do you have that you would like to achieve?
    Think of two and tell your partner.
    - Why are they important to you?
    - What actions are you going to do to achieve them? Make a list.
    - Compare your list with your partner's.
      Can you add more suggestions to each other's notes?

〉 6.6 Project challenge

Project A: A quiz about different jobs

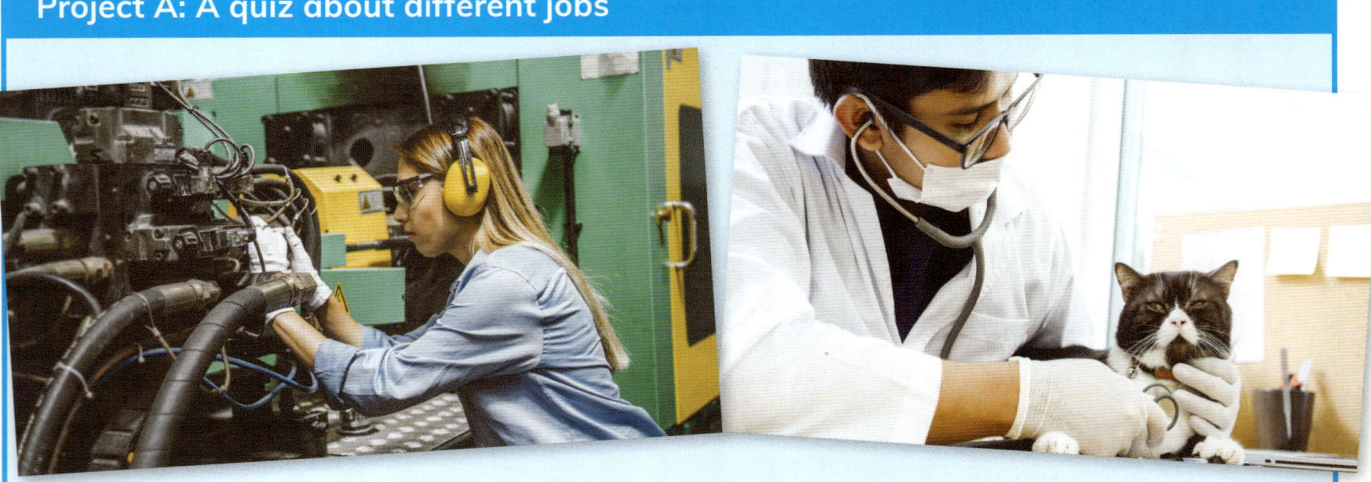

1   Work in pairs or a small group.
    Brainstorm information about jobs in one or two of these categories.

> in your family   in your town or city   in your school

Or choose from different categories of job, for example:

> building   medicine   information technology
> helping people/animals   media   others

2   Write ten clues (two or three for each category) for your jobs.
    Think about:

> qualities and skills needed   activities   uniform   equipment   places

You wear a uniform and a helmet for this job. What is it?
Name two skills a science teacher needs.

3   Write a rough draft of your quiz and check vocabulary, grammar and spelling.

4   Write up your questions and clues on a large piece of paper.
    Include pictures with some of the clues.

5   Swap your quiz with another pair or group to complete.

Project B: A presentation about an inspiring job

1 As a class, discuss jobs that are inspiring to you.

- Who are your real-life heroes? Doctors, nurses, firefighters, police officers?
- Are there any other jobs that inspire you? In the world of theatre, music, art, film or sports? Inventors or other creative jobs?

2 Choose a job to research. Work individually or form pairs or small groups with classmates with similar ideas. Use the internet or library or, if possible, talk to someone who already does this job.

3 Make notes on the following topics:

- A description of the job
- Qualities and skills needed
- The challenges faced in the job

4 Use your notes to write your presentation. If you are working in a pair or group, share the writing of the different parts.
Then proofread each part, check and correct any errors.

5 Find pictures to go with your presentation. Then practise in pairs or small groups.

6 Deliver your presentation to your class. Listen to other presentations. At the end, vote on which job you thought was the most interesting or challenging.

What were the benefits of working together on your project? Were there any difficulties?

⟩ 6.7 What do you know now?

Why do people do their jobs?

1 Which jobs did the people talk about in Lesson 6.1? Which of the words for these jobs are compound nouns?

2 Which job is the uniform designed for in Lesson 6.2? How many features can you remember?

4 What job is described in Lesson 6.3? Write down four personal qualities you need to do this job.

6 What piece of advice is repeated in the poem in Lesson 6.5?

3 Write five sentences to describe your own clothes with any of these features.

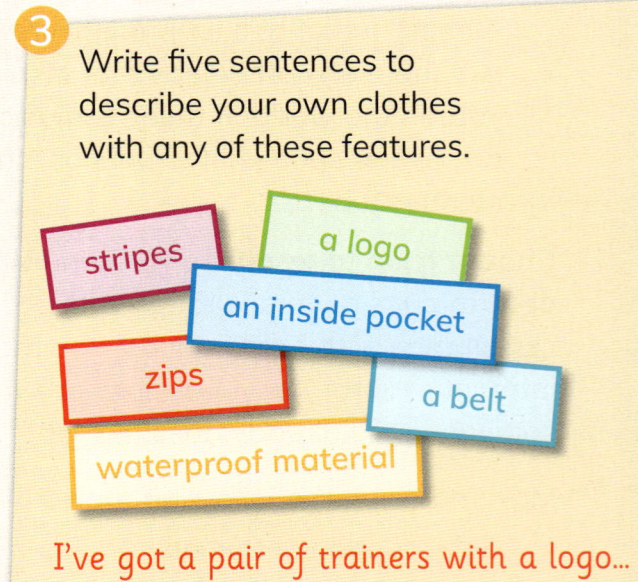

stripes

a logo

an inside pocket

zips

a belt

waterproof material

I've got a pair of trainers with a logo...

5 Which jobs are advertised in Lesson 6.4? Write two sentences for each job to describe the ideal candidate.

He/She is really good at...
He/She is fascinated by...

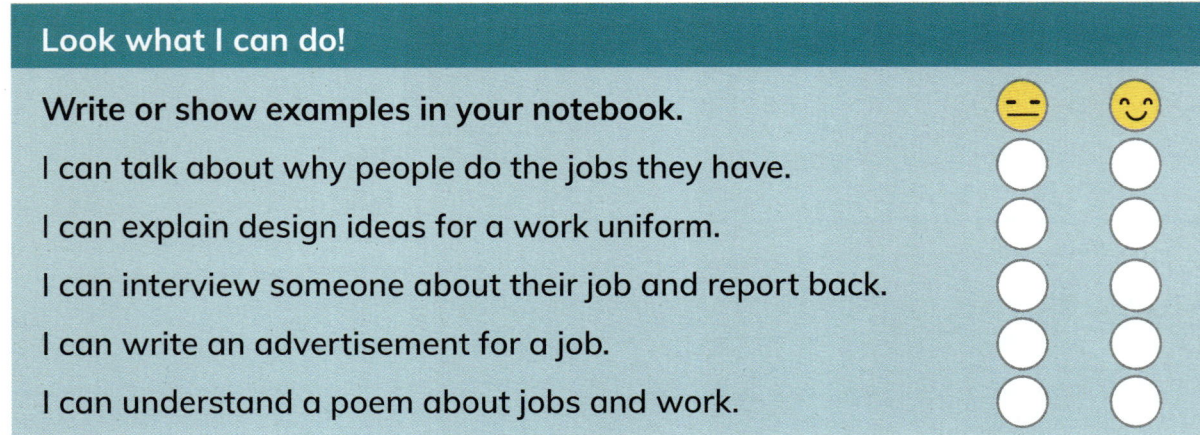

Look what I can do!		
Write or show examples in your notebook.	😑	🙂
I can talk about why people do the jobs they have.	◯	◯
I can explain design ideas for a work uniform.	◯	◯
I can interview someone about their job and report back.	◯	◯
I can write an advertisement for a job.	◯	◯
I can understand a poem about jobs and work.	◯	◯

Check your progress 2

1 Read the clues and solve the crossword. Then put the words into the unit topics:
   4 Inventions; 5 Money; 6 People and work.

Across

2 A machine, controlled by a computer, that does jobs.
3 The symbol of a company.
4 This person uses exercises to treat sports injuries.
7 An animal doctor.
8 An organisation that gives help for free.
9 You can go online, play games and message your friends on these.
11 A type of product made by a company.

Down

1 A device in space used for communications.
5 This person designs machines and engines.
6 To keep money for the future.
10 When you have enough money to buy something.

2 Find six words from Units 4, 5 and 6 and make a revision crossword to test your friends!

3 Work in pairs. Each sentence has an error or a missing word. Take turns to throw a dice and choose the sentence with the same number. Can you correct the errors?

   a I often buy things that I've saved for himself.

   b I am really keen in sport.

   c My friends say that I was good at drawing.

   d At the moment, my friend and I do this activity.

   e In ten years' time, I probably learn to drive.

   f I spend money much carefully if I save it myself.

4 Read the corrected sentences from Activity 3 and tick (✔) the ones that are true for you. Compare with your partner. Which ones are the same?

5 Play bingo! Choose nine verbs from the box and write the past simple form in the grid.

| win | have | buy | save | spend | lose | go |
| get | travel | visit | try | make | do | play |

6 Listen to your teacher. Cross out the past simple verbs you hear in your grid. When you have crossed out all your words, shout 'Bingo!'

7 Work in pairs. Write four true/false sentences about you in the past simple using the verbs in Activity 6. Then swap and guess which of your partner's sentences are true or false.

Last year, I won a singing competition!   Mmm… I think that's false!

8 Work in a small group. Write five future predictions about any topic. Then read them to your class. Vote on the funniest, the most interesting and the one that you all think is the most possible.

In 20 years' time, robots will do all the work in our houses!

9 Compare the stories and poem in Units 4, 5 and 6. Which one did you like the best? Why?

My favourite was… because…

7 Nature's power

We are going to...

- **talk** about what happens in an active volcano using present and past tenses

- **discover** how lightning happens

- **give** safety advice for natural dangers

- **describe** a special place using adjectives and prepositions

- **read** and **enjoy** a poem about the sun.

Getting started

What are the effects of nature's power?

a   What kind of natural events can you see in the photos?
b   What effect do these events have?
c   Have you ever seen or experienced a powerful natural event? What happened?

 Watch this!

〉 7.1 The power of volcanoes

We are going to...

• talk about what happens in an active volcano using present and past tenses.

1 **Talk:** Look at the photos of volcanoes in action.
Who do you think takes these pictures?
What risks do photographers take?

2 **Word study:** Find these words in the photos.

> lava   explode   erupt   crack   ash   crater

3 **Read** the sentences with your partner.
Do you think they are true or false?

a   When a volcano erupts, the river of lava can travel at
    450 km per hour.   true / false
b   If volcanoes erupt near water, they can cause a tsunami.   true / false
c   The temperature of volcanic lava is very, very
    hot – about 200°C.   true / false
d   A volcanic eruption can throw ash 3 km into the air.   true / false

4 **Listen** to the photographer talking about his experiences filming volcanoes. Check your answers for Activity 3.

Use of English – Past continuous

We use the past continuous to describe actions happening at the same time as another action in the past.

We were making a film in Indonesia when the volcano suddenly exploded.

5 **Listen** again and match the sentence halves.

1	We were almost a kilometre away	a	while it was erupting.
2	... we were in the area near the volcano	b	as the earth opened up in huge cracks.
3	Houses were disappearing	c	when the lava was rolling towards us.

6 What is it like to get so close to a volcano, do you think? What can you see, hear, feel and smell?

7 **Listen** to Part 2 and check your ideas in Activity 6.

8 **Listen** again. What good things have volcanoes done for the Earth?

9 **Write:** Are there any volcanoes in your country or region? Find out about the nearest volcano to you. When was it last active? What happened?

- Work in pairs. Imagine you are film makers at the scene of this volcano when it last erupted. Write a description of the scene. Remember to use the past simple and past continuous to describe what happened.

❯ 7.2 Lightning strikes

We are going to...

- discover how lightning happens.

1 Talk: How often do you see lightning in your country?
How do you feel when you see it? How can lightning be dangerous?

2 Vocabulary: Play the Hot Seat game! Act out the words below for
your team mates to guess. You can use definitions, examples and
mimes but don't say the word!

bump into	storm	strikes	electricity	cloud	connect

3 Listen and read about lightning.
Complete the text with the words from the red box.

1 How does lightning happen in a [1] storm ? Lightning is electricity in the storm clouds in the sky. To understand how this [2]_____ is made, first we need to understand how a storm cloud is formed.

2 When the ground is warm, it makes warm, humid air which rises to the sky. When it reaches the sky, the tiny drops of water in the air cool and **form** thunder clouds. At the top of the clouds, the **temperature** is very cold and the water turns into small pieces of ice. The storm winds cause the ice pieces to move around and [3]_____ into each other. This action creates an electric **charge**. The cloud fills up with electrical charges. The tiny ice crystals have a positive charge and rise to the top of the cloud; the bigger pieces of ice have a negative charge and sink to the bottom of the [4]_____. When the positive and negative charges grow very big, a huge **flash** of lightning happens inside a cloud.

3 Sometimes lightning happens between the cloud and the ground. The negative electric charge at the bottom of the cloud attracts a positive charge on the ground and lightning strikes. This positive charge needs a tall object on the ground to [5]_____ with the negative charge in the clouds. So, this is why lightning [6]_____ trees, towers and sometimes even people!

Ice crystals

Key words: physical change

form: make something exist

temperature: a measure of the amount of heat

charge: the amount of electricity that something has

flash: to shine brightly and suddenly

4 Read paragraph 2 again.
Use these words to
complete the diagram.

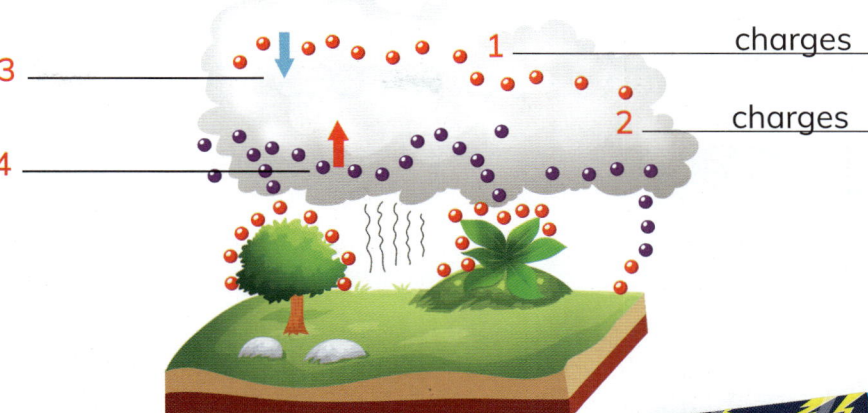

3 _____

4 _____

1 _____ charges

2 _____ charges

hot air	positive
negative	cold air

5 Have you ever seen lightning strike the ground?
Do the Lightning Quiz to find out how to stay safe.

> **When lightning strikes...**
>
> **1** If you are outside and can't shelter in a building, try to shelter...
>
>   **a** under a tree.   **b** in a car.
>
> **2** If you are inside, avoid...
>
>   **a** taking a bath or shower.   **b** standing in the middle of the room.
>
> **3** If you are inside, don't use...
>
>   **a** a landline phone.   **b** a mobile.
>
> **4** You need to stay away from _____ objects.
>
>   **a** rubber   **b** metal
>
> **5** Lightning can set things on fire. It is nearly _____ – hotter than the surface of the sun!
>
>   **a** 30,000°C   **b** 3,000°C

6 **Try an experiment!** You are going to produce **static** electricity.
Work in a small group. You need a balloon, an empty metal
can and a smooth surface.

   a   Blow up the balloon and tie the end.
   b   Rub the balloon against your hair for 10 seconds.
      What does this do?
   c   Now put the balloon near the can. What happens?
   d   Slowly move the balloon away.
      What does the can do?

〉 7.3 Nature's forces

We are going to...

- give safety advice for natural dangers.

1 Talk: What do you know about earthquakes?
Have you ever seen one on TV or in films?
Look at the photos. What can happen?

2 Read: How do earthquakes happen? Read the text
and label the diagram with the words in bold.

Earthquakes happen in places where there is already a break in the Earth's **surface**, called a **fault line**. Under the Earth's surface there are huge blocks of moving rock called **tectonic plates**. Usually the rocks move past each other, but if they get stuck, a lot of pressure builds up. When the plates break free, the pressure is released, causing **waves** under the ground. Then the rock under the fault line breaks and an earthquake happens.

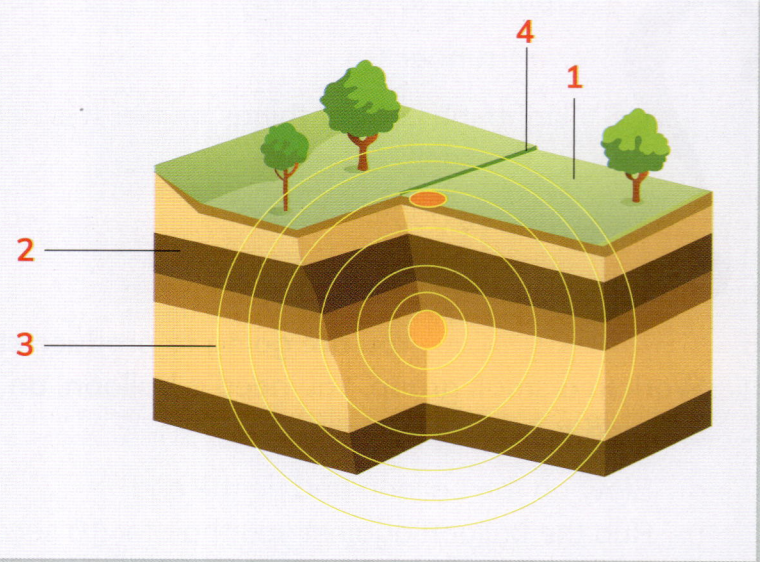

 3 Listen: What do you do if an earthquake happens?
In pairs, write two instructions.
Then listen to the public service broadcast and compare.

4 Vocabulary: Listen to the first part again and act out the verbs of movement with a partner. Then act out the safety advice!

| shake | get down | cover | crawl | hold on |

5 Complete these instructions from the broadcast, using verbs from Activity 4.

¹_____ your head with your arm... ²_____ under a strong table...
³_____ to the table legs until the shaking stops...

6 Use of English: Listen again and complete the sentences with connecting words.

a _____ the shaking starts, get down on your hands and knees.
b Stay inside _____ the shaking stops.
c Don't move from where you are _____ the earthquake is happening.

7 Present it! Create a public service broadcast. Give safety instructions.

Work in a small group. Think of extreme weather or natural dangers that happen in your country or region. Here are some ideas:

| storm | volcano | tornado | sandstorm | blizzard |

- Research why it happens and write a short paragraph.
- Create safety instructions to help people protect themselves when it happens.
- Use connecting words and imperatives. Your instructions must be short and simple, so people can understand and remember them easily in an emergency!
- Make a public service broadcast or podcast and record your instructions. Each member of the group takes a turn to make the recording.

Speaking tip

Giving important instructions

Use **imperative** verb forms to give short simple instructions for important information.

Stay inside... **don't move** from where you are.

Use of English – Connecting words

Connecting words show when something happens

until – up to (a point in time)

as soon as – immediately after

while – at the same time as

〉 7.4 The effects of nature's power

We are going to...

- **describe a special place using adjectives and prepositions.**

1 A special place

In 79 CE, nearly 2000 years ago, **a huge volcano erupted in the south of Italy**. It produced **an ash cloud that was over 20 kilometres high**. It was a poisonous mixture of ash and gas, and, in 24 hours, it covered the city of Pompeii. The temperature of the ash cloud was 300 °C. It destroyed houses and killed thousands of people almost immediately.

> Start with a surprising fact

2 Last summer, my dad and I **visited** Pompeii on our holiday in Italy. Dad said it would be good research for my history project about the ancient Romans. I thought it would be a bit boring! But when we got there, I was really **amazed by** what I saw.

> Past simple

> Adjective + preposition

3 Parts of the city were exactly as they were in the times of the ancient Romans. You can see rows of houses and shops. The ash covered people, animals and objects and turned them to stone. Everything looks exactly the same as it did when the ash hit. So, you can see whole families trying to look after each other. You can also see normal objects that they used every day, like bread, bottles and cooking utensils. These things give us an idea of what life was like in those times. I was surprised by how similar everything was to things we have today.

4 My visit to Pompeii made me feel so many different emotions. I was really interested in the history and information about how the people lived so long ago. I was fascinated by the stone figures of the people, but I felt very sad about them at the same time. Those people must have been so terrified. I felt sad about normal people like you and me doing normal everyday things when something so terrible happened.

1   **Think** of a special place that you've been to. Write as many adjectives as you can to describe it in one minute!

2   **Talk:** Do you know anything about the city of Pompeii in Italy? What happened there? Look at the pictures and try to guess.

3   **Read:** Hannah's description of her visit to Pompeii. What happened there? Were your predictions correct?

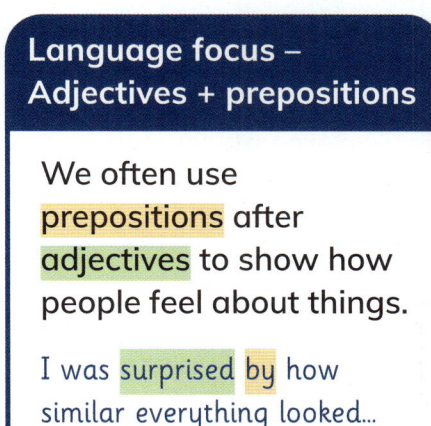

**Language focus –
Adjectives + prepositions**

We often use **prepositions** after **adjectives** to show how people feel about things.

I was **surprised by** how similar everything looked...

4   Read the description again and match each paragraph 1–4 with a heading below.

   a   When Hannah visited Pompeii and who she was with
   b   Her feelings about Pompeii
   c   Interesting or surprising facts about Pompeii
   d   What Hannah saw there

5   **Talk:** Find three interesting facts from the first part of Hannah's description. Which surprised you the most?

6   Match the adjectives and prepositions, then find examples in Hannah's description.

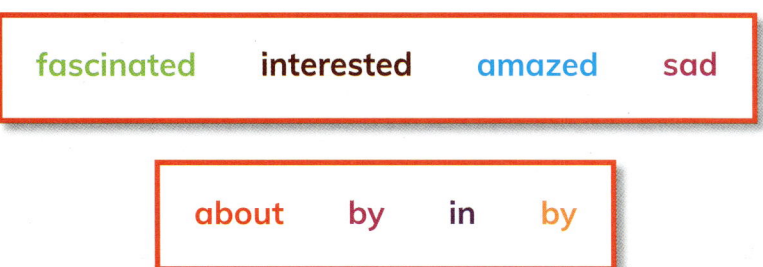

fascinated	interested	amazed	sad

about	by	in	by

7   **Write** a description of a special place.

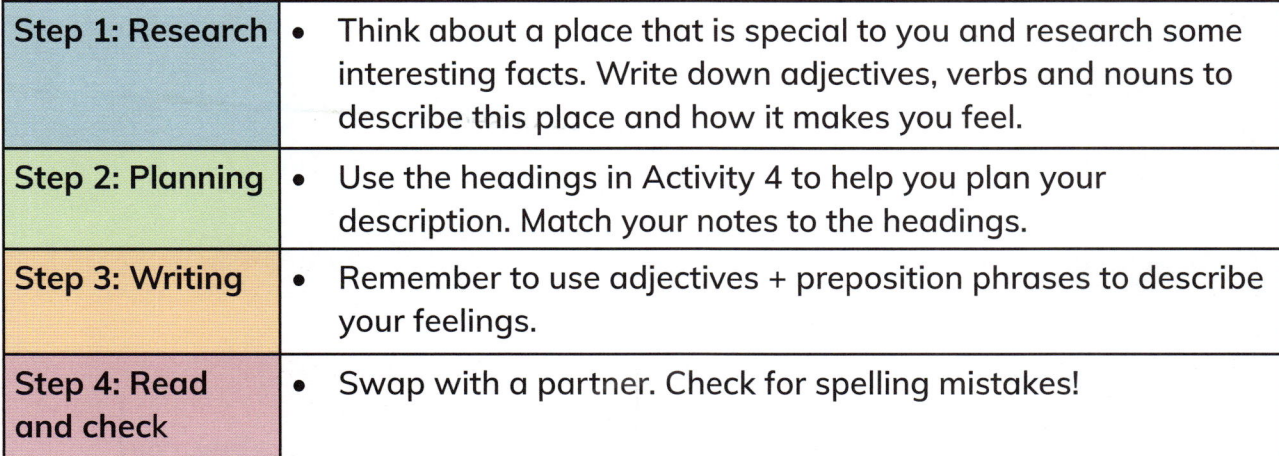

Step 1: Research	• Think about a place that is special to you and research some interesting facts. Write down adjectives, verbs and nouns to describe this place and how it makes you feel.
Step 2: Planning	• Use the headings in Activity 4 to help you plan your description. Match your notes to the headings.
Step 3: Writing	• Remember to use adjectives + preposition phrases to describe your feelings.
Step 4: Read and check	• Swap with a partner. Check for spelling mistakes!

〉 7.5 Thank You Letter

We are going to...

- read and enjoy a poem about the sun.

1 Before you read the poem, make a list or mind map of words and phrases about the sun. What things can you thank the sun for?

The sun

5,000°C

 2 **Read and listen** to the poem. Which of your ideas from Activity 1 are mentioned?

Thank You Letter
by Eric Finney

Dear Sun,

Just a line to say:
Thanks for this
And every day.
Your **dawns** and **sunsets**
Are just great –
Bang on time,
Never late.
On **dismal** days,
As grey as **slate**,
Behind the cloud
You calmly wait,

Glossary
dismal: grey, cold
slate: a type of grey stone

Till out you sail
With cheerful grace
To put a smile
On the whole world's face
Thanks for those
Blazing days on beaches,
For **ripening** apples,
Pears and peaches;
For sharing out
Your **noble glow**;
For sunsets – the
Loveliest things I know.
Please carry on:
We know your worth.

Love from
A Friend on Planet Earth

 3   Read and listen again. Discuss the questions.

a   Find three things that the writer thanks the sun for
     (more if you can).
b   Find words and phrases to describe how the sun looks;
     what it does; how it moves.
c   What kind of country do you think the writer lives in? Why?
d   How do you feel about the sun? Would you thank the sun for
     the same things? What other thoughts about the sun would
     you put in this poem?

Glossary

noble: strong
and brave

4 Word study: Match a word in blue from the poem with a definition.

    a   Very hot and bright.

    b   The time when the sun rises in the morning.

    c   The light that comes from the sun.

    d   The time when the sun goes down in the evening.

    e   When sunlight makes fruit ready to eat.

55 **5 Pronunciation:** Listen and repeat these lines from the poem. Which matching sounds do you hear?

> **Th**anks for **th**ose
>
> **Bl**azing days on **b**eaches

6 Which other lines in the poem have matching sounds?

56 **7** Put the words with the same sound together. Listen and check.

<u>w</u>arm	<u>m</u>agical	br<u>igh</u>t	<u>w</u>onderful	<u>m</u>akes	sh<u>i</u>ning

8 Write a short verse about the sun in your notebook. Use the matching sounds from Activity 7.

Thanks for

Your ____bright____ _____ light

In the morning

Your _____ _____ glow

In the evening

That _____ colours _____

9 **Write** a 'thank you' verse.

- Think of something that makes you feel happy.

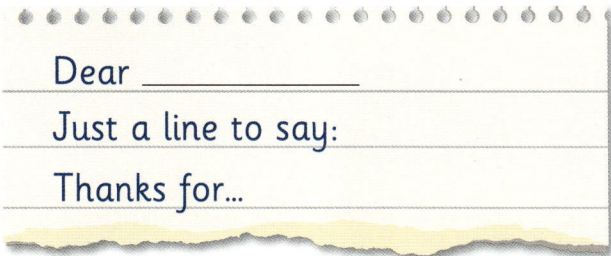

| a person | an animal | an activity | a natural place | a type of weather |

- Choose nouns, verbs, adjectives and adverbs. Put words together with similar sounds. Then put the words together to make descriptive phrases.
- Put the phrases together to make a thank you verse. Start your verse like this (it doesn't have to rhyme); use the example in Activity 8 to help you.

> Dear _____
>
> Just a line to say:
>
> Thanks for...

- Decorate your verse with pictures and make a display. Read other verses and write down two new words or phrases from each one.

10 **Values: Saying thank you.**
What other ways can we say thank you for something? Which do you think is the best way of thanking someone who gives you something or does something special for you?

- Say thank you.
- Send them a thank you card.
- Send them a message to say thank you in another way.
- Be kind to them or another person in the same way in the future.

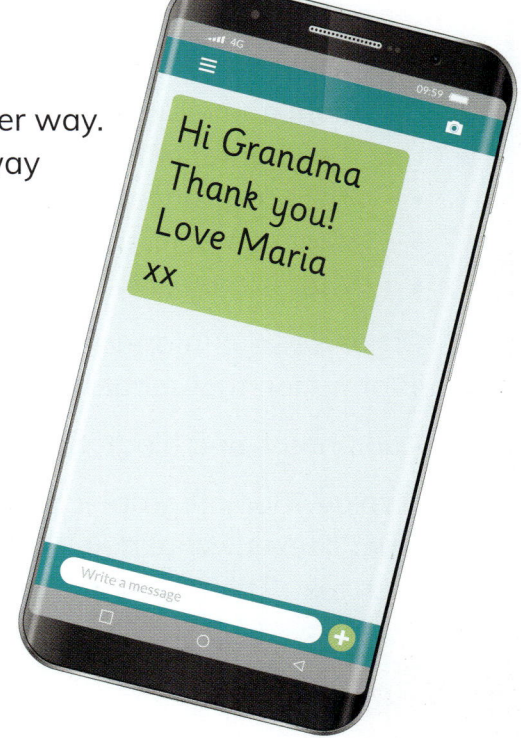

Hi Grandma
Thank you!
Love Maria
xx

› 7.6 Project challenge

Project A: An infographic text about a natural danger

1   Work in pairs or a small group.
    Choose one of these natural dangers and prepare an infographic text.

    > **volcanic eruption   earthquake   tsunami   tornado**
    >
    > **sandstorm   another type of natural disaster (your choice)**

2   Research and make notes. Divide the tasks between you.
    Use the internet or library resources to help you.
    *   What can cause the disaster (e.g. weather conditions, climate change, etc.)?
    *   What can happen when the disaster strikes?
    *   What is the best safety advice?

3   Organise your information into paragraphs. What is the most important
    information that readers need to know? Write short texts with headings.

4   Add photos and diagrams to explain the information on your infographic.

5   Display your infographic texts around your classroom. Walk around and read each
    other's texts. Write down two interesting or shocking pieces of information from
    each text. Then share the information with the class at the end of the project.

Project B: A presentation about a natural disaster

1 Work in small groups. Choose a real-life natural disaster for your presentation. Here are some ideas:

Indian Ocean earthquake and tsunami 2004

Haiti earthquake 2010

Iceland volcano 2010

Hawaii volcano 2018

2 Brainstorm what you know already about the disaster. Then write four questions to find out in your research. Think about:
   - causes and effects of the disaster
   - what happened before and after.

3 Research the disaster using the internet or the library. Use your questions to plan your research. Each group member should take a question to research. Find news reports and photos.

4 Plan your presentation together. Use your questions to organise and write your presentation. Use the past simple and past continuous tenses when you write about the real-life events.

5 Create visuals to go with your presentation. Which visuals will engage your audience and make them want to listen and find out more? Think about:

   videos   sound effects   photos   diagrams/illustrations

6 Check and practise your presentation together, using the visuals. Each group member should present a part.

7 Deliver your presentation as a group to your class, with each group member delivering a part.

What was the most interesting or surprising thing you learned from your project?

❯ 7.7 What do you know now?

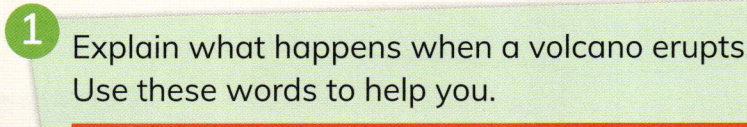

1 Explain what happens when a volcano erupts. Use these words to help you.

| lava | **explode** | erupt | crack | ash | crater |

2 Explain how lightning happens. Imagine you are talking to a younger child.

3 Remember three pieces of safety advice about earthquakes from Lesson 7.3.

4 Finish these phrases to write three sentences about a place you've visited.

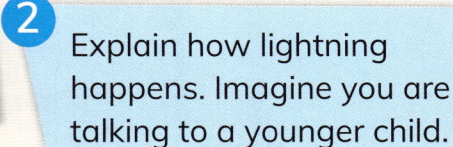

5 Name four things that the writer liked about the sun in the poem in Lesson 7.5. Do you agree?

6 Write five words or phrases to describe the sun from Lesson 7.5.

Look what I can do!

Write or show examples in your notebook.

I can talk about and understand what happens in an active volcano.

I can use the past simple and past continuous to describe an event.

I can explain how lightning happens.

I can give safety advice about a natural danger, using connecting words.

I can describe a special place.

I can describe feelings using adjectives + prepositions.

I can read and understand a poem about the sun.

8 ▶ Entertainment

We are going to...

- **talk** about on-screen entertainment

- **explore** the history of films

- **present** a history timeline using the past simple passive

- **discuss** how to manage screen time

- **create** a storyboard to show scenes from a film

- **read** and **enjoy** a film storyline.

Getting started

How do we use screens for entertainment?

a   What do you think the family are watching in the photo?
b   What kind of things do you like doing at home?
    Do the activities involve screens?
c   Why do you like these activities?
    How do they make you feel?

Watch this!

〉 8.1 Entertainment at home

5

We are going to...

- talk about how we entertain ourselves at home.

1 Talk: What do you like watching or playing at home? Which activities do you spend the most time on? Why?

1

2

3

4

6

2 Play the Dice Game! Roll a dice, look at the number and the activity below next to that number. Talk about...

1 ... a funny video clip online.
2 ... music you listen to.
3 ... your favourite film or TV programme.

4 ... the best book you've read.
5 ... a video game you like.
6 ... your favourite board game.

3 Vocabulary: Which activities in Activity 2 have these features? Which can you see in the photos?

> **characters** actors a plot animation **sound effects** special effects
> **soundtrack** graphics cast costumes setting

4 Listen: Which activity in Activity 2 is Rory talking about? Which features are mentioned in the conversation?

5 Listen again. Name three good points that Rory says about his video game.

6 Talk: Why was Rory's mum worried about the game?

- Why do you think she 'still doesn't let (Rory) play it all the time'?
- Why does Rory say, 'But you have to know when to stop'?
- What would your parents say, do you think?

> **Language focus – Participle adjectives**
>
> Participle adjectives end in -ed and -ing.
>
> My mum was a bit worried.
> (-ed = how people feel)
>
> The graphics are amazing!
> (-ing = describes what causes the feeling)

7 Use of English: Can you complete the sentences with the correct participle adjective? Then listen and check.

a That sounds **frightened / frightening**! Is it violent at all?
b OK, that's **interested / interesting**. I can see her point.
c ... it's quite difficult to play and that makes it more **excited / exciting**.
d There's no time to get **bored / boring**!

8 Talk: What do you like doing at home? Answer the questions about you and compare with your partner!
Use vocabulary from Activity 3 and participle adjectives.

- What kind of films or video games do you like?
- Think about your favourite one. What is it about?

  It's about a superhero called... who...

- What kind of things do you like about it?
  Are there any negative points?

  The plot is really exciting... The soundtrack is awesome!

9 Work in a small group. Compare your experiences and ideas.

- List all the activities you do on screens. How much time do you spend per day? If it is a lot, why do you think this is?
- What other things do you like doing at home?
  What activities can you do that are away from screens?

129

> 8.2 The first films

We are going to...

- explore the history of films.

1 **Talk:** How often do you go to the cinema? How else can you watch films? Name all the places – you have 30 seconds!

2 **Read and listen:** What do you know about the history of films? Read and match the words in blue to the pictures.

a

b

c

d

e

f

Films are everywhere. But how did it all start? Let's ask our movie expert!

In 1891, the first **film projector** was invented by the Edison company. It showed moving pictures on a tiny screen in the machine, but only one person at a time could look at it! Then in 1895, an **audience** could watch moving pictures for the first time, and even paid to see them!

From 1907, people watched **silent films** in cinemas on big **screens**. The only sound came from a **pianist** in the cinema. The actors didn't speak, so they used their faces, and their facial **expressions**, to show what was happening in the story. They wore lots of **make-up** to draw attention to their eyes.

These early films were made in **black and white** – it cost just five cents to watch them at a movie theatre. And in 1912, audiences could buy **popcorn** to eat in cinemas for the first time.

Sound first appeared in films in 1927 and these films were called '**talkies**', for obvious reasons! And Mickey Mouse made his first appearance in a film in 1928. Finally, in 1935, the first movies appeared in colour… the modern age of cinema had arrived!

Key words: film in the past

silent films: films with no sound

expressions: the looks on someone's face, showing what they feel or think

black and white: films without colour

talkies: films with sound and dialogue

3 Read again. How many years are mentioned in the text? Why are they important in the history of film? Discuss with your partner.

4 **Use of English:** Read the Use of English box. How do we make a past simple passive sentence? Complete the rule and choose the correct tense.

> **was** or _____ + the
> **past / present form** of the verb

Use of English – Past simple passive

We use this **passive form** to talk about past events. We want to focus on the event, not the person who did it (or we don't know who did it).

These early films **were made** in black and white. If we want to mention the person who did the action, we use by.

In 1981, the first film projector **was invented by** the Edison company.

5 **Create a timeline!** Complete the sentences using the correct form of the verbs. Then match the sentences to the years on the timeline.

> film   ~~make~~   show   play   sell

a The first movie ___was made___ in colour.
b The first moving pictures _____ to an audience.
c Popcorn _____ in cinemas for the first time.
d The first films with sound _____.
e The music _____ by a pianist in the cinema.

1   2   3   4   5
1895 ___   **1907** ___   **1912** ___   **1927** ___   **1935** _a_

6 **Write: Create your own timeline.**

- Choose one of these forms of entertainment and find out about their history.

> television   computer or video games   music players

- Choose five or six key events. Make sentences using past tenses, including the past simple passive. Write the years and create a timeline.

› 8.3 Too much tech?

We are going to...

- **discuss how to manage our screen time.**

1 **Talk:** In pairs, discuss the questions.

   a   How much time do you spend watching or playing something on a screen?

   b   Can you watch as much as you like or are there limits?

   c   What are the effects of too much screen time?

2 **Read** the advertisement. What is it selling?
   Which of your ideas from Activity 1 are mentioned?

TOO MUCH TECH!

**Fact: Many children spend 50+ hours a week in front of a screen.
   10% are addicted to mobile devices!**

Hard truths about screen time!
Too much screen time can…

- make you tired
- make you bad-tempered
- stop you sleeping properly
- stop you being sociable
- distract you from school work
- make you addicted to your device!

Let's unplug! Let's have…

★ more tech-free activities
★ no-tech zones at home
★ no devices at family meals
★ screen-time schedules

We're not saying no tech – just less tech! TechTime is an easy-to-use app for parents who want to limit internet and apps on their children's devices. Manage screen time by…

 3 **Listen** to Mr Stern's class discussing screen-time schedules.
   What is a screen-time schedule?

 4 **Listen** to the children discussing an example of a screen-time schedule.
   How many hours of screen time are allowed in a week?

5 **Listen** again. What have the children decided for their schedule? Can you correct the errors in the summary?

> **Our screen-time schedule – Lola, Kurran and Ali**
>
> a   Hours of screen time per weekend = 11 hours.
> b   The screen time is the same on weekdays and at weekends.
> c   If you have more screen time on one day, you have the same amount on the next day.
> d   Screen time needed for homework is included in the weekly allowance.

 6 **Listen:** What two points do the children add to their summary?

7 **Use of English:** How do you and your family use your screen time? Ask and answer the questions with your partner! Circle the adverbs.

a   How much screen time do you think you spend weekly?
b   What do you normally play or watch on a screen at the weekend?
c   What do you usually watch with your family?
d   Do you sometimes use a device to do your schoolwork?
e   What homework do you have tonight? Which devices can you use to do it?

8 **Present it!** Managing our screen time. Work in a small group. Discuss the children's ideas in Activities 5 and 6. Use the phrases in the Speaking tip box and the time adverbs.

- Would these ideas work for you? What would you change? Does everyone agree?
- Make a summary of your ideas and compare with another group.
- Over the next week, make an electronic diary and record how much time you spend on-screen a day. Then compare with your classmates.
- What other activities do you like doing at home away from screens?

Use of English – Adverbs of time and frequency

These adverbs describe when an action happens. Some adverbs can describe definite (exact) time:

… we've talked today about what you do on your devices…

… you have a limit of one hour of screen time daily…

Some adverbs don't specify an exact time:

I often use my tablet for schoolwork.

Speaking tip

Giving opinions and responding

So what do you think?
No, I think it's better to…
I think that's a good idea.
Me too.
Yes, that sounds right.
I've got one more point to make. How about…?
Great idea!

› 8.4 Creating film scenes

We are going to...

- **create scenes for a film.**

1 **Talk:** What are your favourite film plots?
   How do you think the film makers get their ideas?

 2 **Listen** to the film trailer and look at the storyboard below. What kind of film is it?

> science-fiction   comedy   horror   adventure   drama   action   historical

3 Choose the best title or write your own.

   a **Happy Camping**   b **Big Adventure Weekend**   c **The Sweet Revenge**

4 Match the sentences to a picture or thought bubble on the storyboard.

   a Horis and Boris are fighting again. 'Oh no, not again!' sighed Dad. `Direct speech`

   b At the campsite, Dad and the boys look for a place for the tent. Boris `Reporting verbs`
      has trouble in mind! Dad looks cheerful – he thinks everything is
      going so well!

   c 'I know what will help!' said Dad. `Speech marks and exclamation mark`

   d 'You'll love camping! Just think of all the fun we'll have... putting up
      the tent and cooking in the great outdoors!' promised Dad in the car.

   e 'You can sleep here if you like, Horis. I think that's the nicest spot...' said
      Boris. 'Here, let me make it more comfortable for you,' he sniggered. `Comma`

   f 'Here's a good place for a tent.... hee hee!' laughed Boris, as he
      spotted the ants' nest.

5 **Talk:** What sound effects and special effects could you add to these scenes? Make the sounds!

Why don't we add... to Scene 1?

Let's put a... in Scene 2...

6 **Read** the Writing tip box and add punctuation to the next four scenes. Change **said** to a different verb from the box.

> sniggered insisted (x2)
> sighed whispered

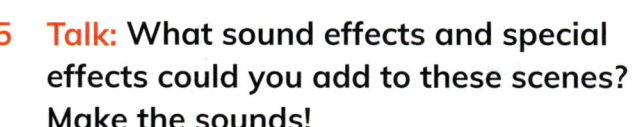

Writing tip

Use direct speech and reporting verbs

Use **direct speech** to make your story more interesting. Use different verbs to show how people said things. Remember to punctuate with **speech marks**, **commas** and **exclamation marks**.

'Here, let me make it more comfortable for you,' he sniggered.

'Oh, no, not again!' sighed Dad.

Scene 7 So that's why he wants me to sleep there... Well, I've got other ideas <u>said</u> Horis.

Scene 8 No, Boris, I insist! I can't possibly take that place. You must sleep there <u>said</u> Horis. No Horis, really, I couldn't... YOU must sleep there said Boris.

Scene 9 Tell you what, boys... I'll take that place <u>said</u> Dad.

Scene 10 Hee hee... serves Boris right <u>said</u> Horis.

7 **Write:** Create a storyboard to continue the story.

Step 1: Ideas and planning	Work in a small group. Brainstorm ideas for three or four scenes and write notes.
Step 2: Writing	Write two or three sentences to explain each scene and include some dialogue. Add ideas for music and special effects too.
Step 3: Drawing	Create a simple drawing for each scene. Don't worry about being a good artist – stick figures are fine. Use colour if you want to.
Step 4: Create a storyboard	Make your storyboard into a poster and display it in your classroom. Read other group's storyboards. Which ideas do you like best?

> 8.5 Jurassic Park

We are going to...

- read a film storyline.

1 **Talk:** What are the best special effects you've seen in films? How do you think special effects are created in films?

2 Have you ever seen the *Jurassic Park* films? What are they about? Why do you think the first *Jurassic Park* film was important in cinema history?

 3 **Read** the introduction to find out. Were your predictions correct?

Jurassic Park is a science-fiction film, based on a novel by American author, Michael Crichton. It tells the story of a group of scientists who visit a very unusual theme park on an island. The park is inhabited by real dinosaurs. During the visit, someone breaks the security code and dangerous dinosaurs escape all over the island. Everyone on the island is in great danger.

The film was made in 1993. It is famous in cinema history because the film makers created very clever special effects using Computer Generated Imagery (CGI) to bring life-like dinosaurs to the screen. After *Jurassic Park*, many other films used the same CGI technology to create fantastic special effects.

4 **Read and listen** to an extract from the novel, *Jurassic Park*.
Tina and her family are on holiday on the island where the story
is set. What strange meeting does Tina have near the beach?

Jurassic Park by Michael Crichton

1 Tina ran until she was **exhausted**, and
then she threw herself down on the sand
and **gleefully** rolled to the water's edge.
The ocean was warm, and there was
hardly any surf at all. She sat for a while,
catching her breath, and then she looked
back toward her parents and the car, to
see how far she had come.

Her mother waved, beckoning her to
return. Tina waved back cheerfully,
pretending she didn't understand.
Tina didn't want to put sunscreen on.
She wanted to stay right here.

Now her mother was calling to her, and
Tina decided to move out of the sun,
back from the water, to the **shade** of the
palm trees. Tina sat in the sand, and kicked the dry **mangrove** leaves.
She noticed many bird tracks in the sand. Costa Rica was famous for its birds.

5 **Read and listen again.**
Answer the questions after each section.

a Where were Tina and her parents?
b Were they sitting together? Where was Tina?
c What did Tina notice in the sand?

> **Glossary**
>
> **exhausted:** very tired
> **gleefully:** happily
> **mangrove:** a tree with
> roots above the ground

2 In the sand, some of the three-toed bird tracks were small. Other tracks were
large, and cut deeper in the sand. Tina was looking at the tracks when she heard
a chirping, followed by a rustling. The **chirping** was probably some ocean bird.
She waited quietly, not moving, hearing the **rustling** again. A few yards away,
a lizard **emerged** from the mangrove roots and peered at her.

Tina held her breath. The lizard stood on its **hind** legs, balancing on its thick tail, and stared at her. Standing like that, it was almost a **foot** tall, dark green with brown stripes along its back. Its tiny front legs ended in little lizard fingers. The lizard **cocked** its head as it looked at her.

Tina thought it was cute. Sort of like a big **salamander**.

d   What kind of animal came out of the jungle?

e   Did it stand on four legs or two?

f   Was Tina frightened by the creature?

Glossary

chirping: the sound a bird makes
rustling: the sound of something moving
foot: measurement of 30 cm
cocked: turn the head sideways
salamander: a type of lizard

3   The lizard wasn't frightened. It came toward her, walking upright on its hind legs. It was hardly bigger than a chicken. Tina thought it would make a wonderful pet.

She noticed that the lizard left three-toed tracks that looked exactly like bird tracks. The lizard came closer to Tina. She kept her body still, not wanting to frighten the little animal. Maybe it expected her to give it some food. Unfortunately, she didn't have any food.

The lizard paused, cocked its head and chirped.

'Sorry,' Tina said, 'I just don't have anything.'

And then, without warning, the lizard jumped onto her hand. Tina could feel its little toes pinching the skin of her **palm**, and she felt the surprising **weight** of the animal's body pressing her arm down.

And then the lizard **scrambled** up her arm towards her face.

g   Was the lizard frightened of Tina?

h   How big was the lizard?

i   What did it do in the end?

6 Talk: Discuss the questions below in groups.

a Do you think the creature was really a lizard?
b What do you think it was? Why?
c What do you think happens next?
d Why do you think the book, *Jurassic Park*, was made into a film?
e Which other stories do you know that have been made into films?
f Which kind of books make good films?

> **Reading tip**
>
> **Guess meaning from context**
>
> If you don't understand a word in a text, look at the other words around it to help you guess its meaning.

7 Word study: Look at the words in blue in the text. Guess their meaning by looking at the other words around them. Choose the correct definition.

		a	b
1	shade	a a place with no sunlight	b a place with lots of leaves
2	emerged	a come out	b go back
3	hind	a front	b back
4	palm	a a part of your hand	b a part of your foot
5	weight	a how tall something is	b how heavy something is
6	scrambled	a move quickly	b bite

8 Pronunciation: Listen and repeat these *th* words from the story. In which words does *th* have a hard or soft sound?

a **th**rew   d **th**ick
b brea**th**   e **th**ought
c **th**e   f **th**en

9 Values: Looking after yourself.
Discuss the questions with your partner.

a Do you think Tina was wise to go so close to the creature? Why? Why not?
b How do you think she felt when the creature jumped on her? How could she have prevented this from happening?
c How can you look after yourself in these places? Give examples.
  • In a city or a place with a lot of people.
  • In the countryside or another natural place with few people.

When you are in a place with lots of traffic, you should...
If you are walking on your own, you shouldn't...

› 8.6 Project challenge

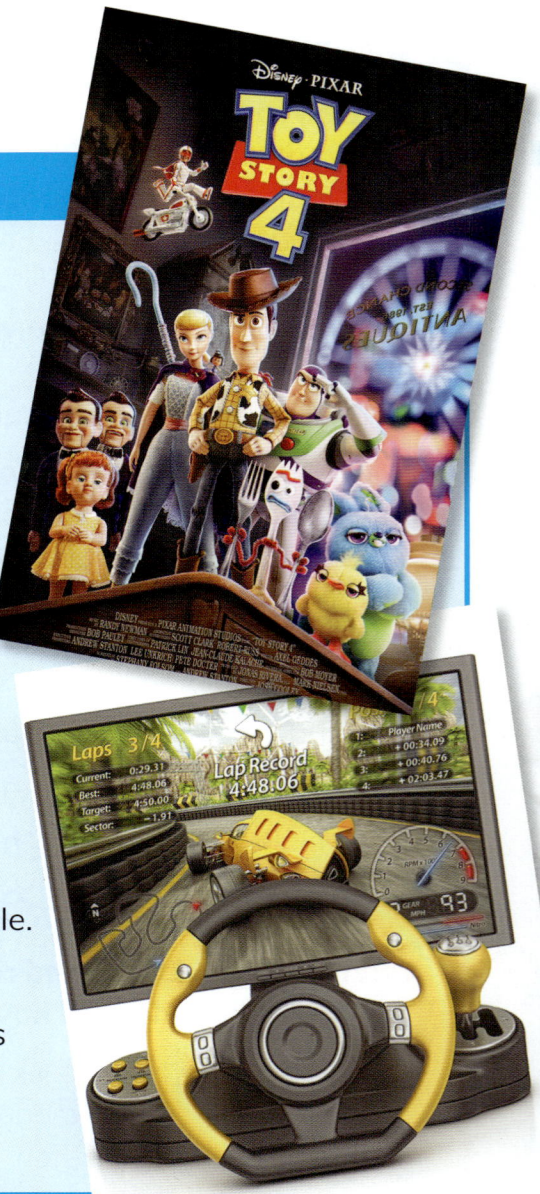

Project A: A film or video game review presentation

1 Work in a small group.
Choose a film or video game to review.
You can review something you liked or didn't like.

2 Use these headings to write notes and organise your presentation.
   - Type of film or video game
   - The plot or storyline (what it's about)
   - The setting
   - Would you recommend it? Why / Why not?

3 Practise your presentation first in your group. Decide who is going to talk about each different section. Remember to start by giving the purpose of the presentation.

   Today, we are going to talk about…

4 Add slides with pictures or a short video clip if possible.

5 Present your film or video game review to your class.

6 Listen to other reviews and write down the adjectives used to describe each film or game. Why did the reviewers use these adjectives?

Project B: Create a film poster and voiceover

1   Work in a small group. Listen to four film trailers, then match to a film type. What other kind of films do you know?

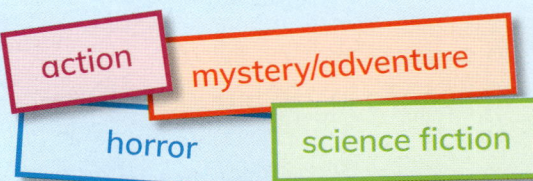

action   mystery/adventure   horror   science fiction

2   You are going to create your own film idea with a voiceover and a poster. Discuss together what kind of films you like watching. Choose a type.

3   Then discuss ideas for a film storyline. Remember that you only need to create a basic story idea. Write notes about...
   - What is the story about? Who are the characters?
   - What is the setting for the story?
   - What problem or dilemma must the characters solve?

4   Write the voiceover. Remember, it must make people interested in the film. You can use sentences or dialogue (or both).
   Use the examples in Activity 1 to help you. Plan your voiceover like this:
   Line 1: Describe the setting of the story.
   Line 2: Introduce a main character.
   Line 3: Ask a question.

5   Practise reading your voiceover aloud and with expression! If you can, include sound effects and background music. When you are ready, record your voiceover (don't say the film title in the voiceover).

6   Now create a title and put in some pictures for your film poster.

7   Display the film posters in your classroom. Now play the voiceovers for each film idea. Can you match each voiceover with a poster?

What responsibilities did everyone have in your group project? What might you do differently next time?

› 8.7 What do you know now?

How do we use screens for entertainment?

1 Write four sentences about your favourite film, TV programme or video game, using participle adjectives.

... is amazing because...

2 In cinema history, what happened in 1895 and 1927?

In 1895, the first... were...

3 Tell your partner about how often you play or watch something on a screen. Use time adverbs.

I watch something on TV for about one hour **daily**.

4 In the storyboard in Lesson 8.4, where does Dad take the twins, Horis and Boris? Why? What plan does Boris have to trick Horis?

5 What is the setting for the story in Lesson 8.5?

6 What happens to Tina at the end of the story?

Look what I can do!		
Write or show examples in your notebook.	😑	🙂
I can talk about on-screen entertainment using participle adjectives.	○	○
I can understand a timeline showing the history of films.	○	○
I can talk about past events using the past simple passive.	○	○
I can discuss how to manage screen time.	○	○
I can create a storyboard to show a film scene.	○	○
I can understand a story that has been made into a film.	○	○

9 Amazing arts

We are going to...

- **talk** about amazing art in public places
- **discover** how music is made from recycled rubbish
- **plan** a day out to discover the arts, using future tenses
- **create** a poem about an amazing building
- **read** and **enjoy** a story about creative thinking.

Getting started

What is the effect of art on us?

a   What examples of art can you see in the photos?
    Which do you like best? Why?

b   What kind of art can you see where you live?
    Where can you see it?

c   Why is art important, do you think?
    What would our world be like
    without it?

Watch this!

> 9.1 Amazing art around us

We are going to...

- talk about amazing art in public places.

1 **Talk** to your partner. Look at the artworks in the photos. In which photo can you see ...

- a **sculpture**
- a **3D** artwork with **metal** and **textiles**
- a **mural** on a wall
- paper flags with a lace **pattern**
- a decorative **doorway**.

2 Each artwork has a purpose or a message. What do you think it is?

 3 **Listen** and match the descriptions to the artworks. Which of your ideas are mentioned?

68

4 **Listen** again to find out the purpose or message of each artwork. Are the statements true or false? Correct the false statements.

a The fish sculpture is made from new materials. true / false
b The big blue decorative doorway shows that it is an important building. true / false
c The artist of the red sculpture wants to remind people to care for each other. true / false
d In Mexico, people decorate the streets with flags every day. true / false
e Before the mural, the metal walls of the World Trade Center site were soft and beautiful. true / false

5 **Vocabulary:** **Types of art and materials. Work in pairs and look at the words. Can you find examples in the photos?**

> textiles   3D   steel   spray paint   mosaic   paper   metal   concrete

6 **Talk:** **Look at the photos. Which works of art do you like best? Are there any that you don't like? Why?**

I like the sculpture because it is…

7 **Read** the Language focus box and choose the correct pronoun. Then tick (✔) the sentences that are true for you. Compare with your partner.

a 'I think art in public spaces is a good idea because **everywhere / everyone** can enjoy it.' ☐
b 'There are art displays **everywhere / nothing** in my school.' ☐
c '**Nobody / Nowhere** in my family likes art.' ☐
d 'There isn't **anywhere / anyone** in my town or city where you can see street art.' ☐
e 'There is **someone / something** in my family who is good at drawing and painting.' ☐

8 **Talk:** **Work in small groups. Choose two of the questions to discuss. Compare your answers with other groups.**

- What kind of art can you see in outside spaces around you? Think about your school, town or city.
- Why do you think artists want to display their work in public places? What advantages are there?
- Is it okay to use art to decorate abandoned buildings and walls?
- Are there any disused spaces or buildings in your town or city? What kind of artwork could make them look better, do you think?

Language focus – Indefinite pronouns

Indefinite pronouns are used to talk about people or things without saying exactly who or what they are, or exactly how many.

… we can make **something** beautiful…

The murals send positive messages to **everybody**…

Anyone who visits festivals in Mexico…

> 9.2 The Recycled Orchestra

We are going to...

- discover how music is made from recycled rubbish.

From trash to treasure

Think for a moment… what can you make from **cans**, wooden **spoons** and **forks**? A violin of course! Welcome to the world of the Recycled Orchestra, a group of young musicians from Cateura in Paraguay. In their orchestra, there is a fantastic selection of **string**, **wind** and **percussion instruments**, all made entirely from **rubbish**.

Cateura is a poor town with mountains of landfill rubbish, dumped from the nearby capital city. It also has a vibrant music school. The rubbish provides musical **instruments** for many local children and teenagers, who otherwise couldn't afford to play. This has transformed their lives…

Ada Rios has played in the Orchestra for many years. She says, 'When I play the violin, I feel like I am somewhere else… I feel transported to another place'.

The music school was started by a man called Favio Chavez, who wanted to improve the lives of the children in this poor community. He understood that music **education** could help the children develop skills of **creativity**, **concentration** and **teamwork**. But when the music school started, there weren't enough instruments for everyone to play. So a local carpenter, Nicolas 'Cola' Gomez, used his **imagination** and made a violin out of bits of rubbish.

Since then, Cola has used old metal tins to make violins, cellos, guitars and drums, and made saxophones and trumpets from old pipes, keys, bottle tops and coins. The instruments cost very little and have given hundreds of children the gift of music.

Since it started, the Recycled Orchestra has gone from strength to strength. It is the **pride** of its community and it has performed many concerts all over South America, playing famous pieces of classical and rock music. Something very beautiful has come out of the rubbish…

Key words: types of musical instruments

string instruments: instruments you play by pulling or rubbing the strings

wind instruments: instruments you play by blowing

percussion: instruments you play by hitting with your hand or a stick

1   **Talk: Look at the musical instruments in the photos. What are they made of?**

 69 2   **Read and listen** to the article about the Recycled Orchestra from Paraguay, South America. Which instruments do they play? What is special about them?

3   **Read the article again and answer the questions.**

   a   Why does the orchestra play instruments made of recycled rubbish? Where does the rubbish come from?
   b   Find six musical instruments. Which are **string**, **wind** and **percussion** instruments? What other types of musical instruments do you know?
   c   What types of music does the orchestra play? What other types of music do you know?
   d   The Recycled Orchestra is the *pride* of their community. Why do you think people are proud of the orchestra?

> **Language focus – Concrete and abstract nouns**
>
> Concrete nouns are things you can see, hear, touch, smell and taste.
> Abstract nouns are not concrete objects. They are concepts, e.g. ideas, feelings and emotions.

4   **Read the Language focus box. Then look at the nouns in green and blue in the article. Which ones are concrete? Which are abstract?**

5   **Talk: Discuss the questions in a small group.**

   a   Do you play a musical instrument? What do you play? What do you like about playing an instrument?
   b   If you don't play an instrument, would you like to? Which one? Why?
   c   How is team work important in an orchestra? What other skills are important?

6   **Use of English: How many examples of the present perfect can you find in the text?**

> **Use of English – Present perfect for unfinished past**
>
> We can use the present perfect to talk about things that started in the past and continue in the present time.
> Ada Rios **has played** in the Orchestra for many years.
> The instruments **have given** hundreds of children the gift of music.

7   **Make a musical instrument out of recycled materials. Work in a small group. What instrument can you make from these waste materials?**

●   How do you make the instrument?   ●   How can you change the sound it makes?

> 9.3 Art attack!

We are going to...

- plan a day out to discover the arts, using future tenses.

1 **Talk:** Have you ever seen any of these artworks? Talk with a partner. How many can you think of?

2 Now play a game with your classmates. Describe an example of art but don't say what it is. Who can guess what it is?

3 **Read** the adverts for cultural events and match each one to a type of art. Which events are inside? Which are outside?

> interesting architecture
> theatre or performance art
> murals   sculptures or statues
> street art   paintings

This has lots of colours and it's next to our playground...

I know, it's a mural – it's called...

Art Safari!

Join our unique city Art Safari this summer! Discover beautiful animal artworks all over our city centre with our exciting Art Safari treasure hunt. Each artwork is created by a local artist and is on show for this summer only. There are sculptures, paintings and even a mural for you to find! All you have to do is download your city map at www.artsafari.com and get hunting!

Art Safari treasure hunts run from June–August. Sculptures are on sale from 1st September.

Star Circus!

Enter our epic world of amazing acrobatics! The Star Circus is back in town, with a theatre extravaganza of daring dance contortion and mesmerising music! Fancy winning two tickets for our opening night? Go to www.starcircus.com, complete the circus quiz and send!

The Star Circus national tour opens on 1st May. Tickets on sale now!

Sculpture Park!

Get creative at the Sculpture Park! Discover our unique collection of contemporary sculpture while you explore the park. Then create your own sculpture using natural materials, in our fun, 3-hour family workshop.

The workshop starts at 2 pm. We meet before in the café at 1.45 pm.

4 Read the adverts again. Answer the questions about the activities in **blue**. Which activity...

a   ... teaches you how to do something? What do you make?

b   ... is a game with clues to find artworks in a city centre. What kind of artworks?

c   ... is a set of questions you answer for a competition? What are the questions about?

5 **Talk** with your partner. Which event would you like to take part in? Why? Why do you think each event includes activities?

 6 **Listen** to Dom's plans for a day out. Which art event is he going to do?

7 **Use of English:** Look at sentences 1 and 2 in the Use of English box and complete the explanation with **present simple** or **present continuous**.

> **Use of English – Present tenses with future meaning**
>
> 1 Their train **leaves** early on Wednesday morning...
>
> 2 They **are arriving** on Sunday and **staying** until Wednesday.

a   We can use the _____ for events in the future which are certain because they are facts, or because there is a fixed schedule.

b   We can use the _____ to talk about the future. It shows that we have already decided something and that we have already made a plan or arrangements.

8 **Listen** and complete the sentences from the next part of the conversation.

a   Then we _____ _____ my mum's friend...

b   After that, we _____ _____ to the Film and Photography Museum.

c   ... The Virtual Experience _____ at 4 pm.

d   My cousin _____ _____ next week – can he come too?

9 **Present it!** Plan a cultural tour or event in your town or city. Work in a small group.

- What kind of cultural things would visitors like to see? Think about things you talked about in Activities 1 and 2.
- What other arrangements would make the day special (e.g. a visit to a cafe, park, other special place)?
- Plan an itinerary. Include an activity to help your visitors get the most out of the event.
- Share with your class. Describe the event, activity and other arrangements. Use present tenses with future meaning. At the end, have a class vote on the most interesting day out.

   The tour starts at...   We're having lunch at...

a

〉 9.4 Amazing architecture

We are going to...

- create a poem about an amazing building.

1 **Talk:** Look at the famous buildings from around the world.
Look at their shapes and colours.
What things do they remind you of?

The Gherkin reminds me of a vegetable!

2 **Read** the poems. Can you match each one to a photo?

b

1

> **Curved wonder**
>
> I look like the sails on a huge white ship
> I am made of smooth concrete and
> gleaming glass
> I am bright, shiny and curved,
> And illuminated at night.
> I look out onto the shimmering ocean
> I am filled with artists, actors and
> musicians.
> What am I? _____

like as a preposition

First person singular

Descriptive adjectives

c

2

> **Mosaic magic**
>
> I look like a magic house in a story book
> I am made of coloured mosaics and
> sapphire glass
> I am wavy, strange and wonderful
> I look out across a busy city
> I am filled with memories.
> What am I? _____

3 **Read** the poems again and answer the questions.

a   What things do the buildings remind the writer of?
b   What materials and colours are mentioned?
c   Why do you think the poems are written using 'I'?

d

4 Now close your eyes! How many images can you remember from each poem? Open your eyes and tell your partner. Which images were the strongest?

5 **Word study:** Can you match the descriptive adjectives in blue with a description?

a The blue colour of a precious stone.
b Something that reflects light in a beautiful way.
c Clean, bright and shiny.
d To light something and make it brighter.
e A rounded shape.

6 **Write** a poem about an amazing building.

Language focus – Uses of *like*

1 **Verb:** I **like** the shape of that building.
2 **Preposition** (+ noun): It looks **like** the sails on a ship. (**to compare two things**)

Writing tip

Plan your work

Take time to think about what you are going to write before you start writing.

Step 1: Choose and imagine	Look at the other interesting buildings in this lesson. Choose one of the buildings to write about. Imagine that the building has a personality. How would it describe itself? Close your eyes and think.
Step 2: Make notes and plan	Now write notes and answer the questions: What do you look **like**? I look like… What are you **made** of? I am made of… What **shape** are you? I am… What is **around** you? I… **What am I?**
Step 3: Writing	Use your notes to write a poem describing your building (don't say its name). Use the **writing frame** in Step 2 to guide you. Use descriptive words. Remember, if you don't know one of the details, invent something! I am filled with memories.
Step 4: Display and read	When you have finished, give your poem to your teacher to make a display. Now read each other's poems. Can you match each one to a building?

151

> 9.5 Willow

We are going to...

- read and enjoy a story about creative thinking.

1 **Talk:** Do you have an art room at school? What's it like? What kind of activities do you do there?

2 **Read and listen** to the story about Willow's art class. What is her art teacher, Miss Hawthorn, like? Why does she get annoyed with Willow?

Willow

by Denise Brennan-Nelson and Rosemarie Brennan

Even on the sunniest days, Miss Hawthorn's art room was cold and dark.

Everything was in its place. There wasn't a single broken crayon in the bunch. The students sat in their rows, silent and still, like eggs in a carton. Except for Willow.

Rosy-cheeked Willow twisted around in her seat, to look out of the window.

"Face forward, young lady." Miss Hawthorn's icy blue eyes **glared** at Willow. Willow **shivered**. Miss Hawthorn's moods were as dark as her clothing.

One day in September, Miss Hawthorn handed out paper, paint brushes and paints. She told her students to make pictures of a tree and hung an example on the board.

All the students painted trees with straight brown trunks and rounded green tops.

Except for Willow.

"Whoever heard of a pink tree?" Miss Hawthorn asked with a **frown**.

"That's what I saw when I closed my eyes," said Willow. A few students **giggled**. Sam snorted. "Pink stinks."

The next week, Willow carried her well-loved art book to school. In it was a picture of a flamingo-pink tree painted by a famous artist.

"Look!" Willow pointed, giving Miss Hawthorn her most magical smile. Miss Hawthorn glanced at the picture, then turned away with a **scowl**.

"Horrid little girl," she muttered, as Willow skipped off.

In October, Miss Hawthorn **passed out** paper, paint brushes and paint. She told her students to make pictures of an apple tree and hung an example on the board.

All the students painted trees with straight brown trunks, round green tops and red apples.

Everyone except Willow.

Miss Hawthorn pointed with a long bony finger. "Look at the mess you've made!"

"And there's no such thing as a blue apple!"

"But that's what I saw when I closed my eyes," said Willow.

Some of the students giggled. Sam laughed especially hard.

"Yeah, whoever heard of a blue apple?"

The next week, Willow carried her well-loved art book to school. She showed Miss Hawthorn a picture of a tree with blue apples. Then she reached into her backpack and took out a blue apple. "This is for you," she said, handing it to Miss Hawthorn.

Miss Hawthorn's face turned **crimson**.

"Horrid little girl," she muttered, as Willow skipped off.

Autumn flew past. Willow always seemed to be in trouble in Miss Hawthorn's class.

"Stop daydreaming, Willow."

"You broke ANOTHER crayon, Willow?"

"Willow! Put that book away!"

Most of all, Willow got into trouble for not painting things in the way Miss Hawthorn wanted her to.

The day before winter vacation began, the students brought presents for their teachers. No one brought a present for Miss Hawthorn.

Except for Willow.

Miss Hawthorn stood by the window and watched Willow and the other students board their buses. She wasn't in any hurry to leave. No one was waiting for her at home.

Miss Hawthorn walked to her desk. She was surprised to see a gift.

No one ever gave her gifts.

"To Miss Hawthorn, my Art Teacher, from Willow."

Miss Hawthorn slowly unwrapped the package. Nestled, in a bed of tissue paper, was Willow's well-loved art book. Miss Hawthorn sat holding the book for a long time.

It was dark outside when she walked towards the cabinet where the art supplies were kept locked away.

Miss Hawthorn filled her arms with paint brushes, paints, colored pencils and a **sketch pad** and carried them to her desk.

She flipped open the sketch pad and stared down at the **blank** page.

Finally, Miss Hawthorn picked up a colored pencil.

For the first time in her life, Miss Hawthorn **doodled**.

Glossary

pass out: give out
crimson: bright red
sketch pad: a drawing notebook
blank: empty
doodled: to draw in a free, informal style

3 **Read** again and answer the questions in pairs.

    a How do most of the students behave in
Miss Hawthorn's art class? Why do you think this is?

    b How is Willow's behaviour different?

    c What does she own, which helps her to think in an
imaginative way?

    d What is Miss Hawthorn's reaction to her?

    e What special gift does Willow give Miss Hawthorn?

    f Do you think the gift will change Miss Hawthorn?
Why? What clue is there in the story at the end?
What do you think will happen next?

4 **Read** the Reading tip box. What do the repeated
sentences tell us about Willow's character?

5 **Vocabulary:** Words that show emotions and
feelings. Look at the words in blue in the story
and match each one to a definition. Look at
other words around the verbs to help you.

    a to laugh in a nervous way

    b a very annoyed expression (on the face)

    c shake slightly (with cold or fear)

    d to look at someone angrily

    e an expression which shows you are annoyed
or confused

> **Reading tip**
>
> **Repetition**
>
> Look out for repeated sentences in stories. These sentences show points and themes that authors want readers to understand in the story.
>
> Except for Willow.
>
> "That's what I saw when I closed my eyes," said Willow.

6 Find other words and phrases to describe Willow
and Miss Hawthorn's characters. Does Miss Hawthorn's attitude
change Willow's character?

7 **Talk:** What do you think of the story?
What message do you think there is in the story?

 8 **Pronunciation: 'i' sounds:** Listen and repeat the words
from the story. How is the 'i' pronounced in each word?
Write the words in the correct column.

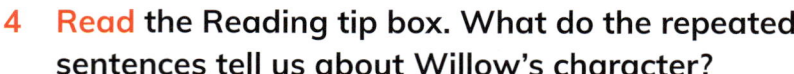

silent   still   icy   twisted   pink   stinks
giggled   skipped   smile   gift

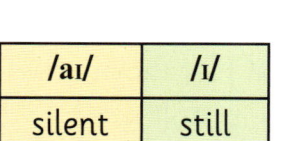

/aɪ/	/ɪ/
silent	still

9 Read the story again. Can you find three more examples of adjective + adjective + noun? Put the adjectives into the correct categories in the table.

Number/ quantity	Opinion	Size	Physical quality (e.g. texture, taste)	Colour	Material	Noun
single			broken			crayon

10 Look at Gabi's list of things she likes painting. Which phrases have adjectives in the **wrong** order? Correct the phrases, then put the words in the correct categories in the table.

A soft furry kitten.   ✓ _____
A red, beautiful sunset.   ☐ _____
Sweet golden fruit.   ☐ _____
A crashing huge waterfall.   ☐ _____

11 Play the crazy captions game!

- Brainstorm adjectives in the categories above, and nouns (any topic).
- In pairs, put the words together to make crazy captions. How many can you make in one minute? (Adjective order must be correct!)
- Choose your favourite crazy caption to read to the class. Then have a class vote to decide the craziest caption!

A fascinating furry telephone!   Lots of huge shiny orange rabbits!

> **Use of English – Adjective order**
>
> We use more than one adjective before a noun, to describe something in more detail.
>
> There wasn't a single broken crayon in the bunch.
>
> The adjectives must be in the correct order (see Activity 9).

12 Values: Thinking in a creative way. How can we build creative thinking skills? Answer these questions in your groups to find out.

- **Trying new things** ✓ When did you last try something new? What new things would you like to try (e.g. a new activity, experience or food)?
- **Problem-solving** ✓ Tell your group about a time when you solved (or helped to solve) a problem. What did you do to find a solution?
- **Finding out new things** ✓ What new things have you learned in this unit? What would you like to find out about now?
- **Stimulating your senses** ✓ What have you made or drawn recently? Have you taken part in any music, dance or drama activities? Which ones do you like best?
- **Reading fiction** ✓ What fiction stories or poems have you read recently? Which ones did you like best? Why?

13 Congratulations! You are developing your creative thinking skills. Why do you think creative thinking is so important?

› 9.6 Project challenge

Project A: Artwork for a public space

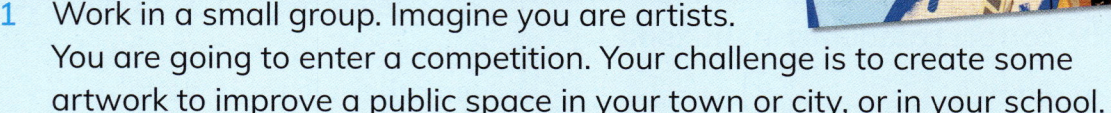

1   Work in a small group. Imagine you are artists.
    You are going to enter a competition. Your challenge is to create some artwork to improve a public space in your town or city, or in your school.
    - Think of a space that is disused or neglected.
    - What does it need to make people want to use it again?
    - What kind of artwork could improve the space?

2   Develop your ideas for your artwork.
    - Gather images from the internet or magazines.
    - What kind of message do you want your artwork to communicate?
    - Make rough sketches to help your ideas develop OR create a collage of 'cut and paste' images.

3   Think about form and materials.
    - What kind of artwork is it, e.g. a painting, mural, 3D sculpture, mosaic...?
    - What kind of materials will you use, e.g. spray paint, metal, glass, mosaic tiles...?

4   Create a poster image of your artwork design.
    - Use a large piece of paper or card.
    - Use paint, pencil, chalk or collage to show your finished design.

5   Present your design to other groups, using your poster.
    Your presentation should explain:
    - Which public space your artwork will improve and why.
    - The message behind the artwork.

    We want to make people feel happy on their way to work...
    We want to make people think about...

6   Which artwork would you like to see in your town, city or school?
    Take a vote as a class to decide the winner of the competition.

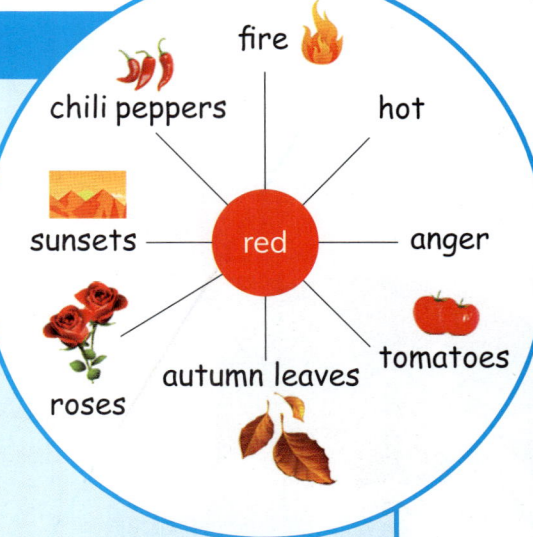

Project B: Create colour compositions about the senses

1. Work in pairs. Choose two colours that you like. Collect interesting images of those colours and create a collage. The images can be anything you like, e.g. food, beautiful landscapes, football shirts, clothes, animals...

2. Make a mind map of all the things that you associate with those colours.

3. Creative writing and art activities often draw on our five senses for inspiration. You are going to use all of your senses to imagine your colours. Look at the ideas on your mind map.

   - What *pictures* do you see?
   - What *sounds* do you hear?
   - What can you touch or *feel*?
   - What can you *taste*?
   - What can you *smell*?

4. Add your ideas to your mind map. Categorise the ideas into sense groups.

   Feel: hot, anger

   Taste: sweet, fresh, spicy, hot

   Sound: autumn leaves crunching

   Smell: wood burning, roses

5. Look at your ideas. Which images do you like best? Which feel the strongest? Circle those ideas on your mind map.

6. Create a composition for each colour, using this writing frame. Use the strongest images from Activity 4. Add extra lines or adjust the structure.

   > Red is *fire, sunsets*. (nouns)
   > It feels *warm* and *angry* and *beautiful*. (adjectives)
   > It sounds like *fire crackling, leaves crunching*. (nouns + gerunds)
   > It tastes *hot* and *spicy*. (adjectives)
   > It smells like *wood burning*. (nouns + gerunds)

7. Present your composition on a poster. Display around your classroom for a gallery walk. Read your classmates' compositions and compare different ideas about the same colours. Note down interesting new ideas.

What were your favourite parts of your project? Why?
What was the most important thing you learned?

❯ 9.7 What do you know now?

What is the effect of art on us?

1 What kind of artworks can you see in Lesson 9.1? Give two examples. What materials are they made from?

2 What are the three types of musical instrument featured in Lesson 9.2? What are the differences between them?

3 What plans do you have for next week? Tell your partner, using the present continuous.

Next week, I'm playing basketball on…

4 Think of an interesting building and describe it to your partner. Can they guess what it is?

It looks like a…   I think it is made of…

5 In the story in Lesson 9.5, where does Willow get a lot of her painting ideas from? Can you remember two images she draws in the art class?

6 Can you remember two 'adjective + adjective + noun' phrases from the story? Who or what do the phrases describe?

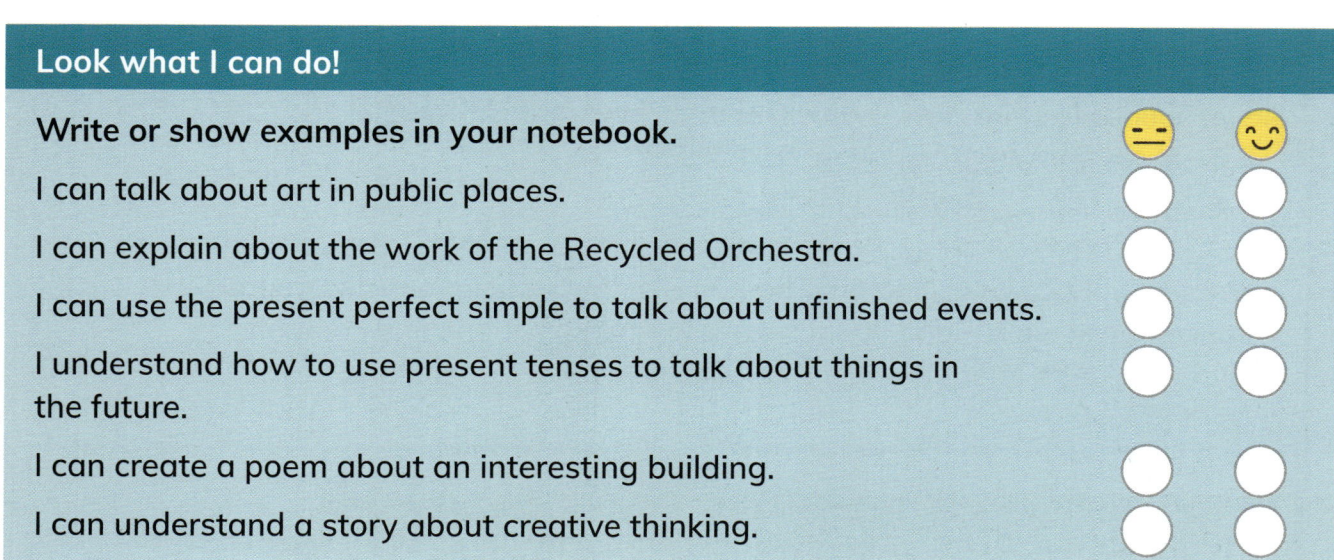

Look what I can do!		
Write or show examples in your notebook.	😑	😊
I can talk about art in public places.	◯	◯
I can explain about the work of the Recycled Orchestra.	◯	◯
I can use the present perfect simple to talk about unfinished events.	◯	◯
I understand how to use present tenses to talk about things in the future.	◯	◯
I can create a poem about an interesting building.	◯	◯
I can understand a story about creative thinking.	◯	◯

Check your progress 3

1 Find four words for each category in the word puzzle.

Nature | Entertainment | Art and design

lava
soundtrack
textiles   audience
creativity   crater   mural   clouds   mosaic
cast
sound effects   tornado

2 Match the definitions to the words in Activity 1.

a the round hole at the top of a volcano

b the people who watch a film or a play

c a large picture on a wall

d the people who are in a film or a play

e the music that is in a film

f the hot, burning liquid that comes out of an erupting volcano

3 Write definitions for two more words and read to the class. Who can guess the words?

4 Play a defining game. Follow the instructions.

a In pairs, choose and write six words from Units 7, 8 and 9. Write them on pieces of paper.

b Hand them to another group, face down.

c One person picks up the first card and gives a definition or a mime to describe the word. The rest of the group guess to try and 'win' the word. The winner is the one with the most words!

5 **Choose the correct answers.**

a While I **was going / went** to school this morning, I saw some storm clouds. ☐

b The special effects in the last film I saw were **amazed / amazing**! ☐

c **Everybody / Everywhere** in my family loves art. ☐

d I have **played / playing** a musical instrument since I was young. ☐

e Next week I **meet / am meeting** my cousins for a day out. ☐

f You can see **old beautiful / beautiful old** buildings in the city where I live. ☐

g I have always been **interested in / on** nature and wildlife. ☐

h There is artwork in our school which was **do / done** by students in
another class. ☐

6 **Tick (✔) the sentences that are true for you. Now compare with your partner.
Which ones do you have in common?**

7 **Roll a dice and answer the question! Work in a small group.
How many points can you score?**

a Name some examples of 'powerful nature' from Unit 7. Which ones can
happen in the region where you live? Tell your group. Do they agree? **8 points**

b Act out four free-time activities from Unit 8. Can your friends guess what
they are? Then tell your group what you like doing in your free time. **8 points**

c Name as many examples of artwork and materials as you can in one
minute (**1 point for each**). Tell your friends which ones you like best.

d Think of an example of a natural danger (e.g. an earthquake) or extreme
weather (e.g. an electric storm). Tell your group two things you should do
if this happens. **8 points**

e Describe or act out something you have watched, read or played in the
last year (e.g. a film, book, TV programme or video game). Can your
friends guess? **4 points**

f Describe a famous building from Unit 9 (but don't say its name). Can
your friends guess? **4 points**

8 **Compare the stories and poem in Units 7, 8 and 9.
Which one did you enjoy the most? Why?**

I enjoyed… the most, because…